FINALLY someone has written a book with a balanced teaching on the hot topic of grace! In the past decade, grace has become the "popular" topic of choice for many preachers. Unfortunately, many have swung the pendulum too far in either direction. For the hyper-religious, grace has a limit. For the lukewarm, grace becomes the excuse for their sloppy lifestyle. But *Graceology* captures the true heart of God as it pertains to His unmerited favor towards us.

This book truly is Josh's life message. In it, he shows us how a personal encounter with God's grace can transform us from the inside out. If you've ever found yourself weighed down by poor performance or asking how God feels about you, the answer is sitting in your hands! Whether you are a veteran believer or merely searching for truth, let the honesty and insight, sprinkled with a touch of humor captured in the pages of this book take you on a journey to discovering the power of God's grace.

–Tim Bittle, pastor of
Youth/Young Adults,
The Father's House in
Vacaville, CA

GRACE
OLOGY

UNFOLD THE GIFT OF GRACE

JOSHUA COPRON

Unless otherwise identified, Scripture quotations are taken from the New King James Version. Scripture quotations marked NIV are taken from the HOLY BIBLE, NEW INTER-NATIONAL VERSION®, Copyright © 1973,1978,1984 International Bible Society. Used by permission of Zondervan. Scripture quotations marked NASB are taken from the NEW AMERICAN STANDARD BIBLE®, Copyright © 1960, 1962, 1963,1968,1971,1972,1973,1975,1977,1995 by The Lockman Foundation. Used by permission. Scripture quotations marked KJV are taken from the King James Version of the Bible. All emphasis within Scripture is the author's own. Please note that certain pronouns in Scripture that refer to the Father, Son, and Holy Spirit, and may differ from some publishers' styles.

To protect the privacy of those who have shared their stories with the author, some details and names have been changed.

DEDICATION

I would like to dedicate this book to my wife, Brynn. This book is the result of your hard work, support, love, and encouragement. We do everything together as a team and this book is no exception. You are a daily inspiration of love and grace.

SPECIAL THANKS

I would also like to acknowledge the team of people that helped bring this book to life: Debra Pines, for your constant encouragement and support, Tom Solomon, for your incredible attention to detail, Colby Pines and Rachel Mansfield, for the hours you invested in editing this book, and Sharon Davis for all "that" you did to prepare it for print. Graceology would not have been possible without your diligent work.

Thank you, Dad, for introducing me to the grace of God. Mom, thank you for demonstrating grace in the way that you've always cared for me. And to Jason Spears, for teaching me to pastor with grace, thank you.

CONTENTS

GRACEOLOGY

FOREWORD

When you walk with someone closely for an extended period of time, you get the privilege of seeing an evolution. I've known Josh Copron for a long time and have had the pleasure of watching him grow into a profound biblical communicator, not only from the platform, but now with the pen. When I got the draft for Graceology, I dove right in, knowing that this subject is his life's passion.

Grace has been a subject most people have a difficult time grasping, especially those within the church. There are those of us who can't stand the thought of anyone getting away with anything. We quickly flash our moral police badges, only to have opinions on everything and everybody. The law rules.

We have been taught to consistently earn what was freely given.

For ancient Jews, when one would bring his sin offering to atone for everything he had done wrong, the offender would have to bring a perfect, spotless offering. When it was presented to the priest, he would go over it with a fine tooth comb to check for the slightest imperfections. Ironically, the priest would never do an inspection of the offender. There was no great inquisition. The fact the offender was bringing the offering in the first place showed, in itself, the understanding sin was present. The two most important parts of the transaction were the realization of the need for atonement for the sin, and the perfection of the offering given to cover it all. If the offering was perfect, then all was made right. The offender knew what was wrong with him. In that moment he needed to know what could be made right. Jesus was proclaimed the Lamb of God who takes away the sin of the world. The perfect lamb. The spotless lamb.

Honestly, how many times have we said or heard Christians say we need to "love the sinner, and hate the sin"? That's nowhere to be found in the Bible. Nowhere. Actually, that phrase was derived from Gandhi's autobiography[00], which he molded from a saying of St Augustine. Jesus never endorsed that way of thinking because it was counter intuitive to everything he taught. Jesus actually removed our ability to even call other people sinners, as if we ourselves aren't one. He chose to call them neighbors. Neighbors are people who come to our assistance when we have gaping wounds. Neighbors are who we find in the ditch having been beaten up by life and left for dead. So, if Jesus had a catchphrase, it would be "love your neighbor, and hate your own sin."

That's why Chapter 6 alone is worth the read. Josh lays out practical insight on how to consistently and "Jesus-ly" love our neighbor. I am confident this book will be illuminating and life giving to everyone who reads it.

–Jason Spears
Speaker, Business Coach

INTRODUCTION

I have a hard time sitting down and talking. If I'm on the phone, you won't find me sitting still somewhere. I can't help but pace around. It doesn't matter whether I'm at my house, my office, or even a store. If I'm talking, I'm moving. The same holds true when I talk to God. In June, 2007, I finished ministry school and moved back home to Las Vegas. Things were paused for me while I waited to hear back about a job opportunity. I was on one of my normal prayer walks when, all of a sudden, God showed me this picture in my mind. I'm a visual person, and God often speaks to me through pictures. On my walk that day, the Lord showed me a picture of a package. It was all wrapped up, but one side of the package was opened. Then God spoke to me in what I call the "Inner-Audible Voice" of God. I didn't hear it with my physical ears, but it was as clear as if someone was talking to me in person: "You have opened up the side of my grace that pertains to salvation, but I want you to unfold the manifold grace of God."

I was a little offended God said this to me because I already considered myself a grace teacher. Most of my messages revolved around the grace and love of God, but at that instant, my entire understanding of grace changed forever. In that moment, God gave me a spiritual download of grace. That's the only way I know how to describe it. Familiar scriptures started flashing through my mind in completely new ways. My entire understanding of the grace of God was made entirely new in fifteen minutes.

As soon as I got home, I looked up the phrase, "manifold grace of God," to make sure I wasn't making this whole thing up. It wasn't a familiar phrase to me, and I didn't even know it was in the Bible. Then I found it: "As each one has received a gift, minister it to one another, as good stewards of the manifold grace of God" (1 Peter 4:10). I spent the next five months doing nothing but studying what the Lord had shown me in that encounter. As I studied, God continued to unfold the message of grace in a way I'd never seen before. Both my life and my relationship with God were completely transformed during that time. I realized I'd been viewing God through the lens of religion, and this was distorting my picture of Him. Seeing the Word of God through this new lens of grace caused religious thought patterns and judgmental attitudes to break off of me, and I fell in love with God all over again.

Through teaching others this revelation of God's grace, I've seen Him do the same thing in the lives of others over and over again. It's because of how I've seen the gospel of grace transform my own life and the lives of others that I've compiled that message into this book. On that same prayer walk, when God first unfolded the gift of grace to me, He also mentioned this would be my first book. Considering I almost failed English, it was quite a shock to hear God say this. My English scores were so low at the time I entered college I had to pass a Remedial English class before I could get into English 101. So it is with great humility, and in obedience to God, that I've written this book. My hope is that the same truth that revolutionized my life will bring you freedom and a renewed love for our Savior.

Graceology is the study of grace. It's a limitless subject. The riches of His grace are immeasurable. Throughout all of eternity we will be discovering the grace and kindness of God (Ephesians 2:4-7). This book is an attempt to unfold another side of the manifold grace of God. As you read, my prayer is you would discover the depths of His grace in ways you never have before. As you journey deeper into His love, may it lead you into an encounter with the God of all grace.

GRACE IS UNEARNED AND UNDESERVED,
WHICH MAKES IT ALL THE MORE
UNEXPECTED.

CHAPTER ONE

WHEN YOU LEAST EXPECT IT

WHEN YOU LEAST EXPECT IT

CHAPTER ONE

Have you ever had something unexpected happen? Where I grew up, there was a water park I used to visit during the summer called, "Wet 'n Wild." If you've ever been to Wet 'n Wild, you know this place had rides, slides, and almost every kind of water-related activity you can imagine. Like most water parks, there was one slide that towered above the rest; its name was Der Stuka. Der Stuka was a body-slide that sat six stories tall. An endless series of steps led to a daunting, 250-foot, nearly vertical free fall. The name Der Stuka comes from an incredibly long German word meaning "dive-bomber." That's what this slide was. This thing generated so much speed they had to build a 115-foot water runway at the bottom just to slow the rider down. It was by far the biggest, scariest, and most intimidating water slide in the entire park.

After waiting several summers, I was finally tall enough to ride Der Stuka. I ascended the spiral staircase, growing more nervous with each step. Six stories seemed like sixty by the time I finally made it to the top. I looked out over the entire water park, and my head began to spin. I thought about backing out, but the six-story walk of shame seemed even worse than any punishment Der Stuka could inflict. I mean, what could go wrong? This was just a slide in a water park. Thousands of people had climbed those same stairs, stood in this same space, and slid down this same slide, and there hadn't been a single fatality - to my knowledge.

I sat down in the cool pool of water at the top of the slide. I crossed my legs, took a deep breath, and gently pushed myself over the ledge. Before I knew it, I was completely airborne. The slide was so steep that, for a brief moment, my entire body was detached from the surface of the slide. I careened through the air toward what was sure to be a watery grave. I closed my eyes and let gravity do its thing, thinking Der Stuka was about to claim its first victim. But, just when all hope was lost, the slide started to curve and my body returned to the surface of the slope. I splashed across the liquid runway before finally coming to a stop. My worst fear was over - or so I thought. When I finally slowed down enough to climb off the slide, something felt wrong. I looked down, and my worries were confirmed. I stared down in a stupor to see that I was completely naked. Apparently, I was flying down Der Stuka with such speed that it ripped my swimming trunks clean off of my body.

In a panic, I started searching for my torn swimming trunks. I looked to my left, then to my right. Nothing. The deceitful suit had abandoned me. Der Stuka seemed to laugh at me as she prepared to propel her next victim down the slope. At that moment, I wished the slide had taken me instead of my trunks. I knew I only had one option: I had to make a mad dash for my things, grab my towel, and cover up as best I could. Unfortunately, my stuff was on the other side of the 30-acre park. That trek is forever engraved in my memory. As I ran through the park, some people stared awkwardly, others laughed. Adults covered their children's eyes as they looked on in horror. Out of all the things I thought might happen when I went on that ride, I never once considered the possibility I might lose my shorts and be forced to sprint naked across the park. It was completely unexpected.

When life throws you an unexpected pantsing by Der Stuka, it's usually not good, but grace is God's goodness showing up when we least expect it and least deserve it. Grace is unearned and undeserved, which makes it all the more unexpected. It's this mystery that makes grace unpredictable. When we feel most unworthy, most undeserving, His grace shows up in our lives. Every time I think, "There's no way God's going to help me get out of this mess," His grace appears.

DEFINING GRACE

When I was in high school, I had to stay after school for some extra tutoring in one of my classes. Luckily, there was a pretty girl that had to stay too, helping make the experience much less painful. One day she happened to mention she needed a ride home. Having recently gotten my driver's license, this was my chance to spend some extra time with her. As we drove to her house, I was so nervous about the girl sitting next to me I didn't notice I was speeding through a school zone. Sure enough, a police officer was right there to clock me going 45mph through a 25mph school zone, which incurred a lovely $200 fine. Now, if the police officer had given me a warning and let me go, that would've been mercy — not getting what I deserve. What if that police office let me off the hook for speeding, and then wrote me a check for $200? *That* would be grace! Unfortunately for me, the reality of the situation was I didn't receive mercy or grace. I received justice. *Mercy* is being spared what you deserve, while *grace* is getting the very opposite of what you do deserve.

MERCY IS BEING SPARED WHAT YOU DESERVE, WHILE GRACE IS GETTING THE VERY OPPOSITE OF WHAT YOU DO DESERVE.

Graceology is the study of grace. In Greek, the word for

"grace" is *charis*. This word is used 147 times in the New Testament. It means "unmerited, undeserved, unearned favor." Grace is God's love, acceptance, forgiveness, righteousness and blessing, that come to us as a free gift through faith in Christ. Grace is best displayed in the darkest places of our lives. Consider this: Jewelers present their diamonds on a black cloth so the shimmering beauty of the diamond is juxtaposed with the dark fabric, causing the diamond to shine brightly against the darkness of the cloth. God's grace is the same. It shines brightest when placed over the backdrop of our own failures. God's grace is greatest in our darkest places.

One of the best examples of this appears in Genesis 20 when Abraham and his wife, Sarah, journey to the land of Gerar. When they arrive, Abraham lies and tells King Abimelech that Sarah is his sister. The king, thinking Sarah is Abraham's sister, takes her for himself. In that moment, Abraham's fear of death silenced his voice. Can you imagine the earful he must've gotten from his wife when it was all over? Not long after all this happened, God came to King Abimelech in a dream and said, "You are a dead man because you've taken this man's wife." Abimelech quickly gave Sarah back to Abraham, but that's not where the story ends. He also loaded him up with sheep, oxen, and plenty of servants. What a picture of grace! Abraham creates this huge mess for himself and everyone around him, and God bails him out. Not only does Abraham walk away unscathed, but he hits the jackpot and receives additional blessings! When Abraham least expected it, God showed up and gave him the opposite of what he deserved - *that's* grace!

When we least expect it and least deserve it, God and His grace show up in our lives. It's easy to think, "If I got myself into this terrible situation, then God won't show up to help me out of it." If that were true, then we'd all be in trouble because most of our problems are the ones we create for ourselves. Trust me. I should know. There was a time in my life when I wasn't exactly living for God. I was trying, but failing miserably. I was always told if you weren't living right, then God wouldn't bless you; that God only blesses those who walk in obedience. During this particular time in my life, I most certainly was *not* living in obedience to God. On top of that, I ran into some financial problems. I didn't have enough money to pay my rent or even my cell phone bill. My refrigerator held only two items: ketchup and mustard. My sad refrigerator and I were days away from being evicted when something unexpected happened: I went out to check the mail, and inside my mailbox was an envelope with no return address. To this day, I don't know who or where it came from, but inside that envelope was a money order for the exact amount of money I needed to cover my rent and cell phone bill.

I'll never forget that moment. I stood at my mailbox, amazed by God's loving grace. I didn't deserve anything from God. I certainly wasn't *expecting* anything from God. As far as I was concerned I had disqualified myself from receiving God's help. But when I least expected and least deserved God's grace, it appeared in the form of a money order. That encounter with grace completely changed me. It made me rethink everything I knew about God. It reassured me God hadn't abandoned me. He was right there with me in the middle of my mess. It's the grace that greets us in our most vulnerable moments that often has the biggest impact on our lives.

One of the best examples of this is in the life of King David. David commits adultery by sleeping with one of his deployed soldier's wives. She ends up getting pregnant, and (in an attempt to cover up the affair) David orchestrates her husband's death on the battlefield (2 Samuel 11). Under the law, David deserved to be put to death, but instead he received grace and forgiveness. The grace of God wiped away David's sin to such a degree that when he is referenced in the Bible, following Him with all of his heart and doing only what was right in His eyes (1 Kings 14:8). Wait a minute! Didn't David commit adultery with Bathsheba and have her husband murdered? And yet the Bible says that David kept *all* God's commandments and *always* did what was right? God's grace so completely forgave David it was as if David's biggest failures never happened. *That* is grace.

Not only did God's grace forgive David, but out of his relationship with Bathsheba (that was never even supposed to happen!), came the next king of Israel, who led the nation into its greatest season of peace and prosperity up until that time. God took the biggest mistake of David's life and used it to accomplish His purpose. That's what Romans 5:20 is talking about when it says, "where sin abounds grace abounds much more." When sin increases, God's grace abounds beyond measure.

To know God forgives us when we sin and mess things up is one thing, but it never ceases to amaze me how God's abundant grace can take our greatest failures and completely turn them around. God is so gracious He will use even our mistakes to accomplish His purpose and plans **IN GOD'S HANDS, OUR GREATEST FAILURES BECOME HIS CROWNING ACHIEVEMENTS.** for our lives. Because of grace, your failures don't derail God's plan for your life. Instead, He seamlessly weaves them into His plan. In God's hands, our greatest failures become His crowning achievements.

I can trace my love for spicy food (and anything in a tortilla) back to my Grandma Francis and the countless hours I spent at her house as a kid. Her walls were always covered in strings of peppers hanging up to dry. Although she would constantly warn us to never touch the peppers, following directions was not exactly my forte as a kid. Grandma's unheeded words of warning suddenly seemed incredibly wise the day my eyes began to burn (and water, and generally feel like they were about to pop out of my skull) after I inadvertently rubbed them with the same hand that had touched the forbidden peppers. (Never, ever, ever again). Despite my burning eyes and a hard, embarrassing lesson learned, Grandma Francis continued to grow the best peppers around. The secret to her exemplary peppers came from the fertilizer she used. After meals, she'd take the scraps of leftover food and put them into a giant garbage can she kept in her shed out back. That can was rotten with the smell of all the stuff we didn't eat, everything that otherwise would have been thrown away and considered good-for-nothing. Over time, the good-for-nothing trash put into that garbage can would transform into rich, lush fertilizer that, when applied to soil, grew huge, succulent tomatoes and peppers. In the same way our unwanted trash yielded deliciousness from my Grandma's garden, it's by His grace that God takes our mess, mistakes, and failures — the garbage of our lives — and uses them to produce His greatest achievements in us. God's grace turns our failure into fruit and our mess into ministry.

BELIEVING IN GRACE

It's much easier to *talk* about grace than it is to believe in it. I think it's often hard to believe in God's grace because we've been conditioned to believe we only get what we deserve. Everything here is based on performance. In our world, you have to work for and earn everything that comes your way. As children, we're rewarded for good behavior and punished for misbehavior. In school, our achievements are rewarded, while our failures might land us (mainly me) in a remedial English course. In sports, we're praised for our performance and scolded if our efforts are sub-par. In our jobs, we're promoted based on how well we produce and reprimanded (or even fired) if we don't meet requirements. In our world, acceptance and love are conditional. They're based on how we behave. Because of this, we're under constant pressure to meet certain expectations or to keep up our performance in order to be loved.

Since almost every aspect of our lives is performance-driven, it's no wonder we often tend to approach God with this same sort of work-based mentality. We believe God relates to us on the basis of our performance. It's easy to see why we live as if He rewards us for our holiness, punishes us for our disobedience, blesses us when we've been good enough, and loves us if we meet His requirements. But grace shows us God is actually the complete opposite. He doesn't love like we love. He loves us unconditionally. He blesses us not because we deserve it but because we realize we don't deserve it. He's continually coming to us and giving us the very opposite of what we deserve. In fact, He's so contrary to everything else in this world, it's often hard to believe God really is that good.

Some people think it's all just too good to be true. They think this concept of grace gives people a license to sin. Let's address this for a moment. In theory, grace could cause someone to think, "Well, if God loves me anyway, then I can just do whatever I want." I love what Dr. Mark Shaw, a missionary in Africa, once said about grace being a license to sin: "The *idea* of grace can lead to sin, but the *experience* of grace never does." The *experience* of grace always causes us to fall more in love with Him. It causes us to lay down our pride and give our lives to the One who gave it all. When you experience the power of grace, it will compel you to live a life that glorifies God rather than one that defies him. In this way, Grace is not a doctrine. It's a person. Those who use the **THOSE WHO USE THE** *DOCTRINE* **OF GRACE AS A LICENSE TO SIN HAVE NEVER ENCOUNTERED THE** *PERSON* **OF GRACE IN JESUS CHRIST.** *doctrine* of grace as a license to sin have never encountered the *person* of grace in Jesus Christ. "Dear friends, now we are children of God, and what we will be has not yet been made known. But we know that when Christ appears, we shall be like him, for we shall see him as he is. All who have this hope in him purify themselves, just as he is pure" (1 John 3:2-3). When you experience Jesus as He is, full of grace and truth, you become like Him. That's why a true encounter with grace (the *person* of Jesus Christ) is not a license to sin but an invitation to a transformative relationship with Christ.

The justice of God was fully satisfied on the cross so He could extend His mercy and grace towards us.

CHAPTER TWO

GOOD NEWS

GOOD NEWS

CHAPTER TWO

My wife collects what she calls, "coffee table books." The collection is basically a bunch of random books, ranging from *365 Ways to Live Green* to a book of Ansel Adams' photographs. There's even one called *What Your Poo Is Telling You*, because, come on - who doesn't appreciate a book with a title like that? On one particular visit to the bookstore, we came across a title that we both knew belonged in our collection: *Church Signs Across America*. The book is full of funny, often cheesy slogans and sayings found on church signs across the country. On one page you might find a sign that says, "Wal-Mart isn't the only saving place in town." Another might read, "Jesus is the rock that doesn't roll." Having lived in South Georgia for almost a decade, my wife and I have found not all church signs are as ridiculously light-hearted as these. Some don't come with a smile and a laugh. In fact, many signs don't reflect a loving or approachable God at all. For instance, I once saw a sign that said, " 'Keep using my name in vain. I'll make rush hour longer.' – God." Think that's bad? They get worse. How about, "You may party in hell, but you'll be the barbecue." Or, how about this old classic: "Stop drop & roll won't work in hell." These absurd, generally misspelled signs don't reflect the good news the gospel is supposed to be. Why is it, at times, the gospel doesn't sound like good news?

The word "gospel", simply means *good news*.[1] This is where the message of God's grace begins. I heard one Bible scholar describe it as, "the nearly-too-good-to-be-true news," which begs the question: why is it there's often more bad news than good being broadcast on our church signs? In ancient literature the word "gospel" appears only a couple of times outside the Bible. This isn't too surprising. After all, there really isn't all that much in this world that's too good to be true. But consider this: if the gospel is the good news about what God has done for us through Jesus, and news serves as an announcement of something that's already happened; then the gospel isn't a call for you to do something, but a declaration of what Jesus Christ has already

THE GOSPEL ISN'T A CALL FOR YOU TO DO SOMETHING, BUT A DECLARATION OF WHAT JESUS CHRIST HAS ALREADY DONE FOR US THROUGH THE CROSS.

done for us through the cross. Therefore, our only job is to believe the good news really is *that* good!

FROM THE BEGINNING

The Bible, from beginning to end, describes a God who loves mankind; a God who is forgiving and merciful. Yet, at the same time, the Scriptures also depict a God who is holy and absolutely just. Exodus 34:7 describes God as one who, "does not leave the guilty unpunished." How then can God be both merciful and just? In order to develop a more accurate picture of grace, we have to rewind the clock to the beginning of time. In the beginning, God created Adam and Eve and placed them in a garden called *Eden*, which means "paradise." God told them they could eat from any tree in the garden except the tree of the knowledge of good and evil. God would come in the cool of the day and hang out with them. Scripture says Adam and Eve were both naked and felt no shame. They got to run around naked, eat organic food, and hang out with God. Does life get any better than that?

God created humankind to live in that perfect world and have a relationship with Him, but Adam and Eve disobeyed God. They ate from the one tree God had forbidden, the tree of the knowledge of good and evil. Because of their actions, sin entered the world and changed everything. Their sin essentially started a ripple effect touching all of mankind. The

Bible states, "all have sinned and fallen short of the glory of God" (Romans 3:23). God is most certainly love, but He's also a God of justice. For God to be just, He can't merely overlook sin, sweep it under the rug, and pretend like it never happened. No one would call a judge who overlooked murder, rape, and violence a just person. For God to be a holy, **GOD IS LOVE,** just, and loving God, He must oppose sin. You **AND SIN** see, all sin violates pure love. Since God is love, **STANDS IN** **OPPOSITION** and sin stands in opposition to love, then sin is **TO LOVE.** also against the justice of God, and justice requires every sin be paid for in full. The Word says, "the wages of sin is death." (Romans 6:23). Therefore, the price and penalty of sin is death.

How then can God forgive us and bring us back into a relationship with Him, while still being true to His justice?

This was our divine creator's dilemma: How can love and justice coexist? How can a holy and just God *justify* those who've sinned? Because God's love was (and is) so passionate, He couldn't allow us to endure the death penalty for our sins. Instead, He sacrificed the only one worthy to take our place: His Son. God allowed the retribution of all of mankind's sin to rest upon the shoulders of His only son. Jesus died on the cross *as* us and *for* us. At the cross, Jesus reconciled love and justice. He wed these two opposing ideas when He shed his blood for us.

Isaiah 53 describes the exchange that took place on the cross in greater detail than almost any other passage of scripture in the Bible:

> *Who has believed our report? And to whom has the arm of the Lord been revealed? For He shall grow up before Him as a tender plant, and as a root out of dry ground. He has no form or comeliness; and when we see Him, there is no beauty that we should desire Him. He is despised and rejected by men, a Man of sorrows, and acquainted with grief. And we hid, as it were, our faces from Him; He was despised, and we did not esteem Him. Surely He has borne our griefs and carried our sorrows; yet we esteemed Him stricken, smitten by God, and afflicted. But He was wounded for our transgressions, He was bruised for our iniquities; the chastisement for our peace was upon Him, and by His stripes we are healed. All we like sheep have gone astray; We have turned, every one, to his own way; And the Lord has laid on Him the iniquity of us all. (Isaiah 53:1-6).*

On the cross, Jesus literally became sin for us. He took upon Himself the sin of all humanity because the righteousness and justice of God required every sin to be paid in full. God took our place, took our sin, and took our punishment. Not only did He take our sin upon Himself, but he also took our grief and sorrow. Strong's Concordance defines *grief*[2] as "anxiety, calamity, disease, and sickness," while *sorrow*[3] is defined as "anguish, affliction, and pain." Therefore, not only did

Jesus take our sin, He also took our anxiety, calamity, disease, sickness, anguish, affliction, and pain. He didn't stop there. He also took the full curse of the law upon Himself. Deuteronomy 28 lists all of the curses that should come **ON THE CROSS, JESUS FULLY** upon a person for breaking the law. But on **SATISFIED THE** the cross, "Christ has redeemed us from the **WRATH OF GOD.** curse of the law, having become a curse for us, for it is written, 'Cursed is everyone who hangs on a tree'" (Galatians 3:13). Jesus became a curse for us so no curse of law would ever come upon you or me.

> *Jesus also took the judgment, punishment, and the penalty of our sin. On the cross, all of God's anger and wrath towards sin was poured out upon Jesus. The justice of God requires that every sin be paid in full, and God didn't cut any corners. In becoming sin for us, Jesus absorbed God's wrath, punishment, and judgment so entirely that - while on the cross - He cried out, "My God, my God why have you forsaken me" (Matthew 27:46).*

First John 4:10 says, "in this is love, not that we loved God, but that He loved us and sent His Son to be the propitiation for our sins." The word *propitiation* carries with it a lot of Old-Testament meaning. Often translated as, "the atoning sacrifice for sin," this word in its simplest form means "the satisfying of wrath." On the cross, Jesus fully satisfied the wrath of God. Through the cross, our sin was punished and the penalty was paid in full. The justice of God was satisfied so He could extend mercy and grace toward us. By justifying us in this way, He could bring us back into a relationship with Him without compromising His righteousness.

> *God presented Christ as a sacrifice of atonement, through the shedding of his blood - to be received by faith. He did this to demonstrate his righteousness, because, in his forbearance, he left the sins committed beforehand unpunished – he did it to demonstrate His righteousness at the present time, so as to be just and the one who justifies those who have faith in Jesus. (Romans 3:25-26 NIV).*

This is the message of the gospel. Most of us have heard it before. Yet, what this message actually means when it comes to our lives here and now is often limited or lost in translation. The major point of the message is this: Thanks to God's infinite wisdom and Jesus' ultimate sacrifice, we can go to heaven when we die. But, what does this do for us here and now in our relationship with God? The answer to that question is found as we continue to unfold grace.

Maybe the reason why so many people don't go to church isn't because they're rebellious but because they feel like God's angry with them.

GOD'S NOT ANGRY WITH YOU

GOD'S NOT ANGRY WITH YOU

CHAPTER THREE

Most of us do not enjoy being around people who are mad at us. If you do, then you may have bigger problems than I'm willing to tackle in this book. As for me, I try to avoid people who have beef with me at all costs.

Grocery shopping is not something I particularly enjoy. One time, making an already miserable trip to the store even worse, I turned down an aisle and spotted a couple who had just recently stopped attending our church because they had an issue with a message I had preached. Before they left the church, this couple made sure to share with me all the reasons why they believed I was wrong. I stood there (surrounded by both literal and metaphorical beef) and remembered how I had tried to discuss the issues they had with my message and reconcile with this couple. Unfortunately, it wasn't a situation in which we could simply agree to disagree. I wasn't mad at them, but I knew they didn't care too much for me. So, being the esteemed man of God that I am, I swallowed my pride, gripped the handle on my shopping cart - and got out of there as fast as I could before they saw me. Don't judge me. We all know you've done the same thing in similar situations.

I'm not sure when it started, but I always thought if God wasn't flat-out angry with me, He was at least extremely irritated with me. I lived with this preconception for years. I don't know if you realize this or not, but feeling like God's angry with you isn't good for your relationship with Him. Nobody wants to be around someone who's mad at them, so if you feel like God's that angry couple in the beef aisle at the grocery store, then you're probably going to react like I did and steer clear of Him. Maybe the reason why so many people don't go to church isn't because they're rebellious, but because they feel like God's angry with them, and they're just trying to keep their distance. Maybe that's the reason a lot of Christians don't pray or read their Bibles. Who wants to enter into that painfully awkward conversation with someone who's mad at them? For the longest time, whenever I sinned, I wouldn't pray or read my Bible because I thought God was angry with me. I thought He wouldn't answer my prayers or speak to me from His word, so I'd wait a couple of days until things cooled down, then I'd start praying and reading my Bible again. Understanding I've been justified and that I have peace with God has given me the confidence to know that God isn't angry with me – not even when I sin.

If Jesus Christ was the propitiation for our sins, and if Jesus satisfied the wrath of God, then that means there's no wrath left for you. There is no more anger towards you. Yet, most of the Christians I encounter on a daily basis still feel like God's angry with them because of some sin they've committed. God doesn't get angry with you when you sin because God released all of His anger towards sin on Jesus when he died. As a believer in Christ, you never need to be afraid of God getting mad at you because all God's anger toward sin has already been satisfied.

"Therefore, having been justified by faith, we have peace with God through our Lord Jesus Christ" (Romans 5:1). Do you realize what this verse means? Because of what Jesus did for you, you now have peace with God. That means God's not mad at you. You and God are at peace because of Jesus. Knowing this could change your life! It changed mine. I mean, if you thought the creator of the universe was mad at you, it would really ruin your day, right? Think about it: if an all-powerful, all-knowing God, who has the ability to make your life miserable, was actually mad at you, well, that's enough to ruin anyone's life, much less their day! So, knowing you have peace with God is really good news.

Every time I teach this, someone comes up to me and says, "What about in the Old Testament when God got angry with Israel for their sin?" I understand why so many people ask about this. It seems only logical that since God gets angry with sin and sinners in The Old Testament, He must get angry with us when we sin. It happened before, so it's bound to happen again, right? Wrong. If you study each instance in the Old Testament when God gets angry, His anger is always directed at the same thing – sin. Because we see God getting angry at sin over and over again in the Old Testament, we think God gets angry with us when we sin, but Romans 5:1 says we have peace with God because we've been justified by faith. To be justified means you stand before God "just as if you never sinned." If you stand before God just as if you never sinned, and sin is the only thing that makes God angry, then God isn't mad at you. You've been justified and declared **IF YOU STAND BEFORE GOD JUST AS IF YOU NEVER SINNED, AND SIN IS THE ONLY THING THAT MAKES GOD ANGRY, THEN GOD ISN'T MAD AT YOU.** righteous by faith, not because of anything you've done or will do but because of what Christ has done for you. That's grace. And man, it's good.

NO JUDGMENT, NO PUNISHMENT

I've had a lot of random jobs throughout my life: I've sold newspapers, cleaned office buildings, waited tables, stocked groceries, washed cars, made thousands of beverages at

Starbucks, and I was even a night security guard for a while. The latter job came with absolutely no perks, other than the badge. I was given no gun, no mace, no baton, only a phone and the instruction to call the "real police" if I saw anything suspicious. The only job from my past I actually enjoyed was working for the Parks and Recreation Department in Las Vegas. My job was to run recreation programs for kids after school and during their summer break. The job was right up my alley - throwing dodge balls, making up crazy games - that's where my creativity thrives. One fateful day, a kid brought a bag of popcorn as a snack and asked if I could microwave it for him. Being the remarkable role model that I am, I took his popcorn to the room next door, tossed it in the microwave, punched in a few numbers, and returned to the game we'd been playing. What I thought were mere moments, turned out to be multiple minutes. Soon, the smoke alarm disrupted our game. Realizing what had happened, I ran to the kitchen to pull out the popcorn. For whatever reason the sight of the slightly burned bag wasn't enough to assure me this popcorn was truly the source of the smoke detector's alarm. I pulled the corners of the bag open to inspect the kernels and released a mushroom cloud of smoke. It was as if I'd accidentally detonated a popcorn atom bomb. Smoke billowed out of the bag and into the rec center as tiny toddlers ran frantically around the hazy gym. As I looked out upon the mass of hysterical children disappearing into clouds of smoke against the backdrop of the deafening fire alarm, it was like a scene out of a war movie -

only the soldiers were children, and I was their shell-shocked leader. The thing about working in a city government building is that, once an alarm is triggered, response teams are immediately dispatched. I sat outside with the evacuated kids in a state of total embarrassment. Fire fighters approached me and gave sarcastic instructions on how to properly prepare popcorn. Needless to say, my boss was absolutely furious. The entire building smelled like burnt popcorn for over a week. Unfortunately, I received daily reminders about how I was incapable of using a microwave. From that day forward, no one was allowed to make popcorn anymore, and I lived out the remainder of my days there forced to go by the nickname "The Kernel." I'm sure the smoky tale of "The Kernel and his Kids" is still told somewhere in the halls of the Las Vegas Parks Department.

Many Christians feel like God is holding their sins over their head the same way my boss held the popcorn incident over mine. They feel as if God's so focused on the mistakes of their past that he can't meet them in their present and prepare their future. Know this: God isn't judging you for your sins or your past because Christ has already been judged. You can't be judged for the same sin Jesus was already judged for. In our modern world that's the law of "Double Jeopardy." Double Jeopardy states that someone can't be tried for the same crime twice. The same goes for the Kingdom of God. You'll not be judged for the same crime twice. Jesus was judged so you'll never have to be judged for your sin.

But he was pierced for our transgressions, he was crushed for our iniquities; the punishment that brought us peace was upon him, and by his wounds we are healed (Isaiah 53:5 NIV).

I used to live in constant fear God was going to punish me for my sin. I viewed every bad thing that happened to me as God's retribution for my failure. Jesus was punished so there will never be a day when I have to wonder if God's going to get even with me for what I did. God doesn't punish us for our sin because Jesus took the punishment for us once and forever. Once you accept this grace-filled truth, it's much easier to live and rest in a relationship with God.

PUNISHMENT AND DISCIPLINE

After hearing this good news, a lot of people tend to ask about the "chastisement of the Lord." Their relief is replaced with nagging questions about things they've been taught and scripture they've read. If this is you, then let's take a moment to clear things up with Scripture. Hebrews 12 says: "My son, do not despise the chastening of the Lord, nor be discouraged when you are rebuked by Him; for whom the Lord loves He chastens, and scourges every son whom He receives" (Hebrews 12:5-6). Okay, so this makes it sound like God's an abusive father who severely punishes those He loves, right? Thankfully, it's the complete opposite. Here's why:

The Greek word for "chastening" is *paideia*. This word provides the root for our word *pediatrician*. It means "education or training; disciplinary correction: - chastening, instruction, nurture."[4] Outside of Hebrews 12, this word is used twice more. 2 Timothy 3:16 uses it by saying, "all scripture is given by inspiration of God, and is profitable for doctrine, for reproof, for correction, for instruction in righteousness." Before I looked into the original Greek terminology used, everything I learned about the word chastise led me to believe it meant to scold, reproof or correct, but here it translates as "instruction." The other time it's mentioned in Scripture is Ephesians 6:4, "And, ye fathers, provoke not your children to wrath: but bring them up in the nurture and admonition of the Lord" (KJV). In this passage it translates as "nurture."

So, the two other times this word *paideia* (for us "chastening") is used, it translates as a nurturing instruction. Yet, for us, this meaning is lost in translation. We've taken that word and those passages to mean punishment. There's a big difference between *loving discipline* and *severe punishment*. Webster's Dictionary defines *punishment* as, "suffering, pain, or loss that serves as retribution; a penalty inflicted on an offender."[5] Punishment is a penalty that's imposed on someone, intended to inflict pain for past acts. Punishment seeks justice.

Discipline, on the other hand, is totally different. Webster's defines *discipline* as, "training that corrects, molds, or perfects the mental faculties or moral character."[6] The goal of discipline is to create self-control and character. When loving parents

DISCIPLINE IS DRIVEN BY LOVE. WHERE PUNISHMENT SEEKS JUSTICE, DISCIPLINE HOPES TO CULTIVATE CHARACTER. discipline their children, they aren't trying to make the children suffer for what they did. The parents are trying to use a mistake as a means to motivate. They're investing their time and instruction in hopes that the discipline will produce a better person. Discipline is driven by love. Where punishment seeks justice, discipline hopes to cultivate character.

Now, when you're being disciplined, it's often hard to tell the difference. When my Mom would punish me, her weapon of choice was a belt. After moving to the south, I learned that the tool for discipline here is often a switch (a firm but flexible stick). Thankfully, I never had to make the long trek to a tree to "pick my switch." However, being spanked by my Mom was the worst, thanks to her terrible hand-eye coordination. Her aim was brutal. While most kids can toss on an extra pair of underwear or something, I had no escape. She'd miss more times than not, and wind up hitting my legs. Despite my mom's flawed aim, my parents always made it clear why I was being disciplined. Before anything else happened, they'd always sit me down and explain to me why I was about to be disciplined. For me, the talk was worse than the actual spanking. Most of the time I'd break down and cry before they even had a chance to spank me. Words are often the most useful tool for discipline. I believe words are definitely God's primary tool for disciplinary correction. His written word is certainly profitable for instruction but so are the words He speaks to us in the present. If we take a moment to meet with Him and truly listen, then God will speak nurturing words of encouragement in order to help instruct us.

Let's take a look at a piece of Scripture where Jesus talks about how God instructs and disciplines His children. In John chapter fifteen, Jesus says, "I am the true vine, and My Father is the vinedresser. Every branch in Me that does not bear fruit He takes away; and every branch that bears fruit He prunes, that it may bear more fruit. You are already clean because of the word which I have spoken to you." (John 15:1-3).

So, Jesus says "every branch that does not bear fruit He takes away." In this passage, *takes* away means "to lift up." My mentor, Jason Spears, taught me when a vine doesn't produce fruit, it's usually because it's fallen down into the mud. A good vinedresser doesn't just cut off the fallen vine; He cleans it and lifts it up closer to the sun, giving it the chance to grow. When we fall into sin and stop producing fruit, God doesn't cut us off. In fact, He does the opposite. He's a good vinedresser, so He cleans us up and pulls us closer to Him. He uses His word to clean us, pick us up, and prune the bad parts off of our lives. Just like a loving parent, He uses His word to discipline us. It's funny - God's discipline is so loving, gentle, and life-giving it's actually nice when He disciplines us. So, remember God never deals with His children on the basis of punishment because all the punishment for sin was poured out on Jesus. Instead, our heavenly vinedresser lifts us from our filth, cleans us off, and holds us in the light of His Son.

UNCONDITIONAL COVENANT

> For a mere moment I have forsaken you, but with great mercies I will gather you. With a little wrath I hid My face from you for a moment; but with everlasting kindness I will have mercy on you,' says the Lord, your Redeemer. 'For this is like the waters of Noah to Me; for as I have sworn that the waters of Noah would no longer cover the earth, so have I sworn that I would not be angry with you, nor rebuke you. For the mountains shall depart and the hills be removed, but My kindness shall not depart from you, nor shall My covenant of peace be removed,' says the Lord, who has mercy on you. (Isaiah 54:7-8).

This verse prophesied the New Covenant God made with man. After the flood, God made a covenant with Noah that He'd never destroy the earth with water again. Do you believe that? Do you believe God's promise He'll never destroy the entire earth with water again? In the same way God swore He'd never flood the earth again, He swore in the New Covenant He'd never be angry with you or rebuke you. It's written, right there in the book of Isaiah, God promises kindness and mercy in the place of wrath.

This New Covenant is extremely similar to the covenant God made with Noah. Noah's covenant was an unconditional covenant. It's a promise that, no matter what, God wouldn't destroy the earth with water. There weren't any stipulations to the promise; there's no fine print or terms and conditions to sign. God didn't say, "If you guys don't make me angry, I won't destroy the earth." No, it's an unconditional covenant that, no matter what mankind did, He'd never flood the earth like that again. In the same way, the New Covenant is an unconditional promise He'll never be angry with you or rebuke you. Regardless of what you do, no matter what happens in life, His covenant of love, mercy, and kindness will always be with you. This covenant of peace will never expire. No matter what happens, we're at peace with Him.

WE CAN REST IN AN EVERLASTING COVENANT THAT IS NOT BASED ON OUR PERFORMANCE, BUT ON THE FINISHED WORK OF JESUS CHRIST.

The wrath and justice of God have been totally satisfied, so we can rest in an everlasting covenant that is not based on our performance but on the finished work of Jesus Christ. The only question is will you believe the report about what God has done through Jesus? Will you accept Him and His good news? Will you believe in God's promise to you? It may sound too good to be true, but that's why it's called the gospel.

P.S.

Not only is God not mad at you, God is not disappointed with you either. Disappointment is the result of unfulfilled expectations. You expect someone to act in a certain way towards you, and when they don't, you're disappointed. God doesn't have any unfulfilled expectations when it comes to you because He knew everything you were going to do before you did it. God isn't surprised when you blow it, so He isn't disappointed in you. I know when you made your promise to God to never commit that sin again you actually thought you were never going to commit that sin again. So you were disappointed when you failed but God already knew you would fall short, so He is not disappointed. In fact, since He knew you would blow it, He took that very sin and laid it upon Jesus so you can have confidence God is not mad at you, and He isn't disappointed in you either.

No one wants to be in an abusive relationship. Luckily for us, God's not an abusive father.

CHAPTER FOUR

HE LOVES YOU... BUT HE MIGHT KILL YOU

HE LOVES YOU... BUT HE MIGHT KILL YOU

CHAPTER FOUR

Isaiah 53:4 assures us "He has borne our grief and carried our sorrows; yet we esteemed Him stricken, smitten by God, and afflicted." As I mentioned earlier, those two words *grief* and *sorrow* mean pain, heartache, calamity, anguish, anxiety, affliction, sickness and disease. That's a bunch of bad wrapped up in two already awful words. The good news is this passage of Scripture says Jesus "bore" and "carried" all of these terrible things for us! When Jesus was nailed to the cross, He took it all upon Himself. This means God isn't the one causing all the grief and sorrow in our lives. He isn't the source of pain. It's physically, spiritually, and scripturally impossible for him to be the source of any of that. So many Christians live under the idea that God is the source of all their problems. Even I used to think He was causing all these terrible things to happen in life in order to teach patience or holiness.

Think about how often we seem to project blame on God. When someone loses a child at a young age, well-meaning Christians say, "God did this for a reason," or, "His ways are higher than our own." In an effort to comfort those who are hurting (which is admirable), people end up inadvertently spreading bad theology. God didn't kill your child. He didn't turn your power off or thrust you into some financial crisis. He's not the source of your grief, and He's certainly not responsible for your pain. Whenever I speak on this misconception, a particular story I once heard comes to mind. It's about a nine-year-old boy who had tragically lost his father. Attempting to make sense of the matter and console the boy, a pastor told him, "God needed your father more than you did, so He took him." I'm sorry, but God didn't do that. That's crazy talk. Despite popular belief, God's not some puppet master in the sky, pulling strings, manipulating our hearts for some unforeseeable "greater good." Countless people have turned away from Christianity because they experienced some similar tragedy, only to have a Christian tell them God did this for some greater good. It's not right, and it's not true.

This sort of thing destroys the revelation of God's love and grace, so let's see if we can't put this myths to rest. First, think about the message we send when we say that kind of "greater-good" stuff. "God loves you, but He'll kill you and your family to teach you a little patience." Think that's too extreme? How about this: Let's say you have a son. Now, this boy of yours falls down the stairs and gets hurt. After making sure he's okay, you take the opportunity to talk to your child about the importance of not playing on the stairs. I've got no problem with that. Your kid, in his limited judgement and foresight, chose to recklessly play on the stairs, like regular kids do. You rushed over, picked him up, brushed him off, and turned something bad, something painful, into an opportunity for your child to learn and grow. That's good parenting. Now, let's say you saw your kid playing on the stairs, snuck up from behind, and pushed your child down the stairs in order to teach him the importance of being careful. That, my friends, is child abuse. It doesn't make any sense to inflict pain on the ones you love in order to force-feed them a lesson. That's just sadistic. Yet this is exactly how many people view God. I've got some good news: God isn't an abusive father. He's not a masked man standing on the stairs waiting to push you down for the sake of a lesson.

It's easy to see how flawed this sort of logic is whenever it's laid out in an anecdote like the one above, but it's much more difficult when we're actually faced with real tragedy. I can remember one night when my wife and I were giving a student of ours a ride home from church. This student explained how her mom was struggling with depression after suffering a second miscarriage. She was going through a real, tangible tragedy. In the midst of this, her mom felt God was testing her to see if she'd remain faithful to Him. I can't tell you how heartbreakingly sad and utterly false this notion is. The idea that God is behind every circumstance in our lives builds barriers between the heart of God, our Father, and us, His children. This theology rests at the root of so many contentious relationships with God. How many people have abandoned their faith and turned their backs on God because they think He's some sadistic deity? And really, who can blame them when Christians are spouting "greater-good" one-liners in the midst of tragedy? But, consider Romans 8:28 for a moment: "And we know that all things work together for good for those who love God, for those who are called according to His purpose." God promises that no matter what negative things may befall us in life, He'll always take those things and transform them for good. This can easily be misconstrued to mean God is, indeed, behind these bad things, but that's not at all what it means. It means, while not everything happens *for* a divine purpose, everything does happen *with* a divine purpose. God isn't behind the crap in our lives, but if our lives happen to be filled with crap, He knows how to make some incredible fertilizer.

GOD ISN'T BEHIND THE CRAP IN OUR LIVES, BUT IF OUR LIVES HAPPEN TO BE FILLED WITH CRAP, HE KNOWS HOW TO MAKE SOME INCREDIBLE FERTILIZER.

Remember *grief* and *sorrow* also include sickness and disease. Rest assured then, the cross also accounts for these things. Isaiah 53:6 says, "by his stripes we are healed." On the cross Jesus certainly died for our sins and sorrows, but He also died for our sickness and disease so we might experience healing. This verse goes for ALL healing! Whether we need emotional, physical, or spiritual healing, Jesus made it available to us through the cross.

"When evening had come, they brought to Him many who were demon-possessed. And He cast out the spirits with a word, and healed all who were sick, that it might be fulfilled which was spoken by Isaiah the prophet, saying: 'He Himself took our infirmities and bore our sicknesses.'"(Matthew 8:16-17). Jesus quoted this passage of Scripture right after healing all those who came to him sick or ill. When Jesus died on the cross, He bore your sickness and your disease so you could be healed. So, if Jesus bore your sickness and disease, then God isn't the one making you sick. He can't possibly be the source of sickness if He took care of it on the cross. God doesn't give people cancer to teach them patience or to help them become more holy. If we were to cast the same sort of blame on our earthly fathers that we do on our Heavenly Father, Child Protective Services would show up. Remember, He's not an abusive father. Think about it. If any single entity caused all of the grief, suffering, pain, sickness, and disease in the world, no one would want to enter into a relationship with that entity. Yet we wonder why so many people turn away from God. No one wants to be in an abusive relationship. Luckily for us, God's not an abusive father. Therefore, we have to stop viewing Him and portraying Him as such.

I WILL NEVER LEAVE YOU

As a young boy, I thought when I sinned, God left. In my mind, Jesus packed up His suitcase, sprouted some pretty sweet wings, and said, "Sayonara!" to my heart. Even though many might not admit it, I think a lot of us tend to live under this false, often juvenile, pretense. When we sin, He bails, but once we repent, He's back. Jesus isn't some vagabond, abandoning hearts and homes on a whim. You see, Jesus was forsaken so that, even when we sin, God will never forsake us. Just before His death Jesus cried out, "My God, my God, why have you forsaken me?" God forsook Jesus so you and I never have to be forsaken. No matter what happens in life, no matter what we might do, there will never be a time when God forsakes us. This may seem like I'm making light of sin, but if we think God leaves us each time a sin is committed, then aren't we making light of His sacrifice?

"For He Himself has said, 'I will never leave you nor forsake you'" (Hebrews 13:5). The New Testament was written in Greek. Greek is a complex language, far more expressive than English. When you translate from Greek to English, you often lose a lot of the original meaning. The Greek is such a rich and beautiful language that it is often too difficult to translate one word in Greek to one word in English. Thankfully for us, The Amplified Bible considers the original Greek meaning when translating to English. One of my favorite verses in The Amplified Bible is Hebrews 13:5: "He himself has said, I will not in any way fail you, nor give you up, nor leave you without support. [I will] not, [I will] not, [I will] not in any degree leave you helpless, nor forsake nor let [you] down (relax My hold on you)! [Assuredly not!]." There are some things we just can't translate into English with a single word. Look at the emphasis on "I will not, I will not, I will not, I will not." Just in case you missed it, God assures us FOUR times He'll neither leave nor forsake us.

It's passages like this that make me stop and wonder whether or not this is all too good to be true. The funny thing is, *it is* too good to be true. That's the very reason it's called the *gospel*. God isn't angry with you. Even when you sin. He's **ANY AND ALL** no longer judging you for your sin because **PUNISHMENT FOR YOUR** it's already been judged in Christ. Any and **SIN WAS LAID** all punishment for your sin was laid on Jesus, **ON JESUS, SO** so there's no punishment left for you. God's **THERE'S NO PUNISHMENT** a good God. He's a great father who is in no **LEFT FOR YOU.** way, shape, or form causing the pain and heartache in your life. Rather, He took it all upon Himself, so that you could experience emotional, physical, and spiritual healing. He's not the cause of your grief or sorrow. Instead, He's constantly planting seeds in the soil of our pain. No matter where you find yourself in life, know He's with you and He'll never leave. His presence, forgiveness, and goodness in your life have nothing to do with you or your performance. It's all because of the finished work of Jesus. He finished it, and that's good news!

You can't experience God's love for you
and be afraid of Him at the same time.
Fear and love are incompatible.

CHAPTER FIVE

DRIVING OUT FEAR

DRIVING OUT FEAR

CHAPTER FIVE

When I was in my early twenties, I lived in a little Texas town called Sherman. I didn't have much at the time. Everything I owned fit inside of my tiny apartment. My apartment complex, Woodridge Apartments, was fondly regarded as "Hoodridge." Granted, these were the cheapest apartments you could find in Sherman, Texas, so the place definitely earned its nickname. My then-girlfriend lived on one side of the complex, while I lived on the other. Her apartment faced this old, abandoned lot where a decrepit building sat, withering away. Apparently, the old building had been a mental institution in the 1920s. This place was straight out of a horror movie. It was beyond creepy. The place's hazy past sparked all sorts of stories. Locals claimed that cults snuck into the building late at night to sacrifice animals and perform wild rituals. Needless to say, my girlfriend was seriously sketched out by this place, and I was glad my room didn't face the old asylum.

One night my girlfriend and I were hanging out at her apartment when she asked if she could borrow my car. It was getting late, but she needed to go to the store to get some things. I gave her my keys and told her I'd just walk back to my apartment. She took the keys and I left for my apartment. Now, what she didn't know was that I didn't walk back to my apartment. Instead, I ran out to the car and climbed inside. I unlatched the back seat so I could push it down from the trunk. Then, I climbed in the trunk and waited. After what seemed like a lifetime, she finally climbed into the driver's seat. With the abandoned asylum in sight, she started the engine. Just before she put it into gear, I erupted out of the trunk and jumped towards her. Her face went white and she froze in fear. Her terror lasted only a moment before she realized it was me. Her white face turned red with rage as her fists flailed in my direction. To this day, I haven't seen total terror transform into riotous rage quite as quickly as it did for my girlfriend that night. In that moment, any love she had for me collided with absolute fear, creating a vortex of confused anger. In this chapter, I want to look at the connection between love and fear as they pertain to our relationship with God.

FEAR OF PUNISHMENT

*And so we know and rely on the love God has for us.
God is love. Whoever lives in love lives in God, and
God in them. This is how love is made complete
among us so that we will have confidence on the
Day of Judgment: In this world we are like Jesus.
There is no fear in love. But perfect love drives out
fear, because fear has to do with punishment. The
one who fears is not made perfect in love. (1 John
4:16-18 NIV).*

At the age of seven I accepted Jesus Christ as my Lord
and Savior. I understood that He died for me so that I could
go to heaven. Although I became a believer at a young age,
I didn't really grow up attending church regularly. While my
church attendance was sporadic at best, I tried to read my Bible often and pray regularly. During the brief time I spent in
church, the main thing I picked up from other Christians was,
if I lived according to the rules, God would bless me. If I broke
the rules, then God would punish me. Those
two sentences summarize the majority of the
messages I heard at a young age. My inter-
pretation was as basic as the message: do
right, get blessed. Do wrong, get punished.

**WORKS-BASED
FAITH LED ME
TO LIVE IN
CONSTANT
FEAR OF GOD
PUNISHING ME.**

Even as a child, this works-based faith led me to live in
constant fear of God punishing me. In church services I'd raise

my hands for salvation, believing God was going to send me to hell because I had sinned the week before. As a teenager my misconceptions worsened as I became more aware of my shortcomings. I couldn't escape my failures and my inability to live up to God's standards. With every sin committed, I'd wait for something bad to happen to me and, most of the time, something negative would eventually happen. For instance, my car would break down, and I'd see it as God punishing me for one of my many sins. It may sound strange, but a lot of the time I'd be glad when these bad things would happen. I was relieved when tough times struck because I wasn't waiting for the punishment anymore. Sometimes the fear that comes from anticipating punishment is worse than the punishment itself. So, my life went like this: I struggled with my inability to live up to God's perfect standards, then waited in agonizing anticipation for God to get even. Something bad would eventually happen, and then I'd chalk it up to God getting back at me for some sin I must've committed. Then the whole cycle would start over. Lather, rinse, repeat. Sin, fear, punishment.

Occasionally I'd sin and nothing bad seemed to happen. If a couple of days went by and no hardship came, then I just figured God chose to show me mercy. For some reason I had this idea that when I sinned, God had five days to get even with me. If nothing bad happened during those five days, then He must have let that one slide. This now seems silly, and it's a dangerous way to live. Going through life like this makes it all too easy for us to blame God for any and every bad thing that may happen in life.

Of course, I wasn't the only person who lived this way. When I was in my twenties, I taught a small, home Bible study. A handful of people would gather each week to hang out and dig into the Word. I had a friend named James who always attended the Bible study. So, when James didn't show up one week, I gave him a call to make sure he was okay. When he finally picked up the phone, his response was priceless. "Sorry," he said, "I couldn't make it this week. God blew out one of the tires on my car." There was a split second where I thought I must've misheard him. "Wait," I said, "did you say that God blew out your car tire?" Without hesitation he responded, "Yeah, I forgot to tithe this week so God blew out my car tire."

All I could picture was an angry God, perched high in heaven, with a sniper rifle. Just when James' car came into view, He pulled the trigger, nailed the tire, and blew the vengeful smoke from the barrel of His godly gun. As it turns out, James had grown up in a church that really emphasized tithing. They taught him God was going to get the money one way or another. If you didn't tithe, He'd take your money through unexpected hospital bills, car expenses, or some other inconvenient cost. One way or another, God was going to get that money. Sadly, this isn't an over-exaggerated account of what a lot of churches teach and what even more Christians believe.

Like many others, I once lived in constant fear of God punishing me because I seemed to mess up more times than not.

The more I tried to live for God the more I seemed to miss the mark. I had to pray and read my Bible every day or face the vengeful wrath of God. Adhering to harsh guidelines was impossible, so I was never good enough, and I soon realized that I never would be. I was constantly aware of all my inadequacies, and this caused me to live in a perpetual state of fear, never knowing what God might do to me next.

So, in the midst of all this fear and self-loathing, I was confronted by this verse: God's "love has no fear, because perfect love expels all fear. If we are afraid, it is for fear of punishment, and this shows that we have not fully experienced his perfect love," (1 John 4:18 NLT). This spoke volumes to me. I realized I was living in fear of God punishing me because I didn't realize how much He truly loved me. His perfect love leaves no room for fear in our lives. We're not supposed to live with the crippling fear God's going to punish us. And if we do, then we haven't fully realized how much He loves us.

Almost every single time I teach on God's love, people tell me they already know He loves them. Whenever this happens, I feel obligated to ask a few questions: Do you fear God will punish you when you sin? Do you feel like the bad things that happen to you are a result of God getting even with you, or testing you? I give them a moment to digest these questions but almost every time the answers are "yes." If that's what you believe, then you haven't fully grasped God's love for you because a true understanding of God's love drives out all fear.

FEAR OF THE LORD

Now, you might be thinking something like, "Aren't we supposed to fear God?" Let's talk about this for a moment. What about all of those verses in the Bible about "the fear of the Lord"? For example, Proverbs 9:10 says, "the fear of the Lord is the beginning of wisdom." Deuteronomy 6:13 talks about fear too: "You shall fear the Lord your God and serve Him." Many people read these verses and think they're supposed to be afraid of God, but the verses telling us to "fear the Lord" aren't referring to us living in fear of God's imminent punishment.

So, if the "fear of the Lord" doesn't mean we're supposed to be afraid of God, then what does it mean? We could debate an answer to this question all day, but I think Jesus might be the best source to define the "fear of the Lord." In Matthew 4, Jesus is in the wilderness being tempted by the devil. The devil tells Jesus he'll give Him all the kingdoms of this world and their glory if He'll fall down and worship him. "Then Jesus said to him, 'Away with you, Satan! For it is written, 'You shall worship the Lord your God, and Him only shall you serve.'" (Matthew 4:10).

Jesus answers the devil by quoting from Deuteronomy 6:13. Deuteronomy says "You shall fear the Lord your God and serve Him." But, look at what Jesus did when He quoted this scripture. He changed the word "fear" to "worship." Jesus said to fear God is to worship Him. In the Old Testament, the word for fear means "respect, reverence, astonishment, awe, and honor." So, if we take the Old Testament's definition and combine it with what Jesus said to Satan in the desert, then "fear of the Lord" becomes an awe and respect for God that produces love and worship.

Let's apply this understanding of what "fearing the Lord" means in other verses. "In the fear of the Lord there is strong confidence, and His children will have a place of refuge." (Proverbs 14:26). How can you have strong confidence in someone who frightens you? It doesn't make much sense. That's why the Amplified Bible says, "In the reverent and worshipful fear of the Lord there is strong confidence, and His children shall always have a place of refuge." When you are in awe of how great and mighty God is, it gives you confidence to face everything life throws at you. That's what the fear of the Lord is! It's an awe-inspired, reverent worship of God.

FEAR ISN'T ABOUT COWERING AT THE PROSPECTS OF PUNISHMENT; IT'S ABOUT WORSHIPPING GOD FROM A PLACE OF RESPECT AND HONOR.

Look what happens when we apply this newfound definition to a verse from the Psalms. "If You, Lord, should mark iniquities (keep record of our sins), O Lord, who could stand? But there is forgiveness with You, that You may be feared" (Psalm 130:3-4). If you translate the word "fear" as literally being afraid of God, then this verse doesn't make any sense. God's forgiveness and mercy don't make us afraid of Him. Rather, they cause us to love and worship Him. Fear isn't about cowering at the prospects of punishment. It's about worshipping God from a place of respect and honor.

FEAR AND PERFORMANCE

You can't experience God's love for you and be afraid of Him at the same time. Fear and love are incompatible. If you don't believe me, then find that old girlfriend I scared outside of the insane asylum! She will tell you. Many people think the opposite of love is hate, but it's not. The opposite of love is fear. And when you understand and experience God's love for you, then there's no place for fear. Fear is living with the expectation of judgment and punishment, two things Jesus endured in our place. The New King James Version translates the word punishment as "torment," and that's exactly what waiting around for God to punish you is. It's total torment! When you understand God's love for you revealed through the cross, it drives out the fear of punishment.

I'm sure you have had someone in your life who has frightened or even terrified you. When I was a kid, I had a basketball coach who terrified me. When this guy would yell, his entire face would turn red. Needless to say, his face was red a lot. He could make the toughest teenagers tear up like toddlers. There was one game in particular when we were winning by 8 points. There were only five minutes left in the game, and I did something stupid to pick up my fourth foul. One more foul and I'd be out of the game completely. Before I got the chance to dribble the ball again, coach pulled me out. As I walked toward the sideline, I could see the vein in his neck sticking out. Any time the vein made an appearance, you knew you were in trouble. He grabbed me by my jersey and threw me into my chair. He put his stubby hand around my neck and let out a thunderous yell that echoed throughout the gym. The eyes of every person in that place turned toward us. Even the guy I fouled stopped shooting his free throws to see what was happening.

The worst part about playing for a coach who yelled at me all the time was how it affected my performance on the court. The more he yelled at me, the more afraid I became of messing up. The more fearful I became, the more I messed up! Fear had a negative affect on my performance. The same is true when it comes to your relationship with God. If you're constantly worrying about some unforeseen, imminent punishment, then God's plan and purpose for your life will never come to fruition.

Consider "The Parable of the Talents" in Matthew 25:

> *For the kingdom of heaven is like a man traveling to a far country, who called his own servants and delivered his goods to them. And to one he gave five talents, to another two, and to another one, to each according to his own ability; and immediately*

he went on a journey. Then he who had received the five talents went and traded with them, and made another five talents. And likewise he who had received two gained two more also. But he who had received one went and dug in the ground, and hid his lord's money. After a long time the lord of those servants came and settled accounts with them. So he who had received five talents came and brought five other talents, saying, "Lord, you delivered to me five talents; look, I have gained five more talents besides them." His lord said to him, "Well done, good and faithful servant; you were faithful over a few things, I will make you ruler over many things. Enter into the joy of your lord." He also who had received two talents came and said, "Lord, you delivered to me two talents; look, I have gained two more talents besides them." His lord said to him, "Well done, good and faithful servant; you have been faithful over a few things, I will make you ruler over many things. Enter into the joy of your lord." Then he who had received the one talent came and said, "Lord, I knew you to be a hard man, reaping where you have not sown, and gathering where you have not scattered seed. And I was afraid, and went and hid your talent in the ground. Look, there you have what is yours." But his lord answered and said to him, "You wicked and lazy servant, you knew that I reap where I have not sown, and gather where I have not scattered seed. So you ought to have deposited my money with the bankers, and at my coming I would have received back my own with interest. Therefore take the talent from him, and give it to him who has ten talents." (Matthew 25:14-28).

Notice how fear affected the servants' performance: The servant who was given one talent took it and buried it in the ground. Out of fear, he hid what was given to him. When the master came to settle accounts, the servant who had buried his talent in the ground told his master the reason he had hidden it was because he was afraid. His fear of the master had a negative impact on his performance. Instead of being productive, he hid the talent in the ground. His fear of failure caused him to do nothing.

Fear often paralyzes us from accomplishing things for God. We can be so afraid of making the wrong choice that we don't do anything. I've had friends who've been so desperate to know whether or not something was God's perfect plan, they were unable to take a single step without 100 percent confidence they were moving in the right direction. I had a friend once who was a powerful and anointed musician and songwriter. When he was offered a position as a worship leader (something he felt was his calling in life), he was so afraid of moving outside of God's will that he never made a decision. What's so sad about this is the very thing he wanted to avoid (missing God's will for his life) is exactly what happened when he refused to move forward. Ten years later he's stuck in the same place doing absolutely nothing with his gift. When you live in fear of making a mistake, you end up wasting your time and talent, just like the disgraced servant in Matthew 25.

FEAR-BASED MOTIVATION

When church leaders use the fear of punishment as a means to motivate believers toward holy living, it doesn't really work.. If you've ever attended any sort of legalistic, or rules-driven church, then you know exactly what I'm talking about. How many people in churches like this actually stop sinning? The only thing legalistic churches accomplish is making their attendees better at hiding their sin. At best, this sort of theology might make people conform for a short period of time, but it won't produce lasting results.

WHEN YOU LIVE IN FEAR OF MAKING A MISTAKE, YOU END UP WASTING YOUR TIME AND TALENT.

One time when I was a kid, I vividly remember thinking I had missed the rapture. (For those of you who may not be familiar with this term, it refers to the belief that before the second coming of Jesus to earth, believers who are alive will be caught up to meet the Lord in the air.) It was one of the most frightening experiences of my life. Early one Sunday morning, as my dad and I drove to church, we pulled into the parking lot and noticed there was only one car (besides our own) in the entire lot. It was almost time for the service to start, and the only two cars there belonged to my dad and the pastor. My mind jumped to the worst possible conclusion: It had happened. The Lord must've come back in the middle of the night, and the only people left behind were my dad, my pastor, and me. In a panic, I started confessing sins I'm not really sure I had even committed. I prayed for Jesus to make a quick U-turn on his way to Heaven and pick me up before it was too late.

In case you're wondering - we didn't miss the rapture that day. We had forgotten to set our clocks back the night before the end of Daylight Savings Time and were an hour early to church. Regardless, I never wanted to feel that way again. So I decided it was time to really start "living right," but my efforts were short lived. Eventually, I fell back into the same old routine of sinning, repenting, and then waiting in agonizing anticipation for judgment to come down from on high. The problem with fear-based motivation is the fear fades away, and we return to life as usual. Fear only produces short-term behavior modification. The message of the gospel isn't about behavior modification. It's about an inward transformation. The only thing able to produce transformation is love, God's love.

In a way this makes perfect sense. Don't we tend to distance ourselves from the things and people we fear, while drawing near to the things and people we love? Think about the relationships you've had in your life. Has there ever been someone like this? Someone you were afraid of disappointing? It could be a boss, a coworker, or even a relative. Think of someone you were afraid of making a mistake around and ask yourself, "Was that a healthy relationship?"

You can't have a healthy relationship with someone who frightens you. When you are petrified of a person the goal of the relationship becomes avoiding punishment. If, deep in your heart, you're afraid of God, then you'll keep Him at a distance. Once you know you're safe and secure in His love, and that you're accepted by Him despite your faults, then you can begin to unload the junk in your life without fear of rejection. Only when this occurs can you truly experience total transformation.

Of course, whenever people talk about removing the fear of God's judgment from their daily mindset, it's only natural for questions to arise: What'll keep people in line? What'll keep people from living in sin? How will we maintain order? Whenever people ask me these questions, my answer is simple: The love of Christ! Fear is a powerful motivator, but it's not greater than love.

And honestly, it's not like fear has really been working all that well in stopping humans from sinning. For instance, have you ever watched someone skydive? As they sit, looking down at the deep, blue sky before the jump, their fear is often obvious. Fear may cause the adventurer to hesitate, but if the jumper's heart is set on skydiving, they'll jump every time. The same goes for the sin in our lives. Fear may cause us to hesitate before we sin, but if our hearts are bent on sinning fear alone will never put an end to sin.

There's no denying fear is a powerful motivator. Thankfully, there's an even greater motivator that has the power to conquer all. Martin Luther King, Jr. preached about it. The Beatles built an empire around it. Whitney Houston sang about it. Even the lady who wrote the *Twilight Saga* knew love is far more compelling and powerful than fear could ever hope to be. If you don't believe me, then experiment with this theory for yourself: (1) Walk up to a woman who has just had a baby. (2) Try to snatch that baby out of her hands. (3) See what happens. It doesn't matter how big or intimidating you are. It doesn't matter how afraid of you she may be. She'll attack you with a force previously unknown to man. Why? Love. Love is the superior motivator. It's more powerful and more compelling than anything else on Earth. That's why fear isn't meant to govern our lives, but instead, the love of Christ is meant to guide us on a daily basis.

FEAR IS A POWERFUL MOTIVATOR. THANKFULLY, THERE'S AN EVEN GREATER MOTIVATOR THAT HAS THE POWER TO CONQUER ALL.

The same grace that saves you is the same grace that sustains you.

CHAPTER SIX

SAVED BY GRACE, BUT...

SAVED BY GRACE, BUT...

CHAPTER SIX

Have you ever received a compliment sandwich? I don't mean a *complimentary* sandwich - those are awesome. I'm talking about criticism disguised as flattery - not so awesome. A compliment sandwich is served when someone tries to pile some deli-cut negative criticism between a couple of slices of fresh-baked compliments. The "meat" in the center of the compliment sandwich is usually what this person *actually* wants to say to you but is afraid to serve it up without the "bread" of flattery on each end. Like this compliment sandwich, I was forced to eat once: "You did a great job teaching today," someone said to me after one of my sermons, "but I really prefer

SAVED BY GRACE, BUT...

deep teaching. You were very entertaining though." That was a tough one to choke down. No matter how kind or flattering those fluffy pieces of bread are, it doesn't make it any easier to consume the "but" that's hiding in the middle. No matter how much they butter you up for the "but", the criticism quickly becomes the focal point of the conversation, and from that point on, it's hard to hear anything else the sandwich-server has to say.

The gospel is often presented as a compliment sandwich: "God loves you, but now you need to live a holy life and follow these rules because Jesus died for your sins. You're forgiven, but God won't bless you unless you follow these rules - Jesus loves you!" Talk about wedging the bad news in between two pieces of sweet bread. The gospel starts to sound like a raw deal when it's presented like this. Think about the common process of becoming a Christian. Most people who have responded to the gospel did so in a church service. You give your life to Jesus, you pray the "sinner's prayer," and you're loved and accepted by a grace-giving God who accepted you regardless of your past sins and failures. But once you become a Christian and start going to church, they hit you with a ton of things you can and can't do in order to maintain your status as a Christ-follower. The rules may change slightly depending on the denomination, but the general outline is as follows: Go to church every week, read your Bible, pray every day, tithe, and do your best to follow God's commandments. Simple enough. But then they slowly start to work in more and more things

Christians shouldn't do: Don't watch R-rated movies, don't listen to this-or-that type of music, don't curse, don't drink, smoke, chew or date those who do. Sure Jesus saved you by grace, *but* if you want to live a life that God will bless you need to follow these rules to stay in God's "good graces."

Why is it God's feelings toward us seem to change after we pray the sinner's prayer? Before we say it, they tell us, "God loves you no matter what you've done." This promise of unconditional love is one of the main reasons most of us say the prayer and choose to believe and accept Christ in the first place. But, after the prayer, there are suddenly all of these conditions to God's love: If you don't tithe, God will curse you; if you don't confess your sins every day, God won't hear your prayers; if you break these commandments, God will punish you. The list goes on, and on, and on. Most Christians understand we're saved by grace, but why is it after the initial prayer, it's all about what *we* must do for *God* in order to keep Him loving us? These "guidelines" tend to lead Christians away from a grace-based faith and into a relationship that revolves around works. Not long after salvation, many people find themselves saved by grace, but living by works.

> *"For by grace you have been saved through faith, and that not of yourselves; it is the gift of God, not of works, lest anyone should boast" (Ephesians 2:8-9).*

I understood salvation was made possible through grace,

but now I was saved, I thought I had to start earning God's love and acceptance through righteous works. I didn't just think I had to earn God's love through good deeds, I also thought if I ever wanted to receive His blessings I had to earn those through works as well. This sort of thinking separated me from the gracious heart of God and turned my faith into more of a duty than a delight. It was like I was walking a never-ending tightrope: One false move and all would be lost. My joy was jaded; my passion for God was replaced by guilt; I lived in constant fear of punishment; and my faith was focused more on my own performance than my relationship with Him. But, when I rediscovered the grace of God, the joy of my salvation was restored. My love and passion for God returned because I began to focus on His love and grace for me, instead of my shortcomings.

"MUCH MORE THEN..."

"But God demonstrates His own love toward us, in that while we were still sinners, Christ died for us" (Romans 5:8). This verse alone sounds great, but it goes on to set up verse nine: "Much more then, having now been justified by His blood, we shall be saved from wrath through Him" (Romans 5:8-9). If God loved you when you were a sinner; when you didn't want anything to do with God, when you weren't trying to live holy, when you didn't care about doing the right thing, then why would you think God somehow loves you less because you messed up? If God's love for you was unconditional when it came to the point of your salvation, then why would there be any reason to believe now (after you've been saved) His love would be dependent upon your actions? His love for us didn't diminish with our sins prior to being saved, therefore His grace will remain steadfast, regardless of our works, after the point of salvation.

You can be the worst Christian on the planet, but God's love for you is still not dependent upon your behavior. In my experience, Christians are good at extending grace to "the lost" but terrible at extending the same grace to a Christian who stumbles. Grace was not intended just for the lost; it's what sustains us in our daily relationship with God.

If an unsaved drug addict walked into the average church, the church would extend grace to him. They'd tell the addict **GRACE WAS NOT INTENDED JUST FOR THE LOST; IT'S WHAT SUSTAINS US IN OUR DAILY RELATIONSHIP WITH GOD.** God loves him, that God has a plan for his life, and regardless of what he's done in the past, God will forgive him. But if that same person comes into the church as a Christian, he's in big trouble. The same church extended grace to the unsaved person would probably tell the Christian God is upset or mad at him. They might say God isn't able to bless him until he "gets right with God." I know this because I've seen it firsthand. I've heard it. I've witnessed churches extend grace to the lost with one hand and berate the fallen Christian with the other. The church desperately needs a revelation of grace goes beyond just salvation. We need to understand the "much more then" grace and mercy that's available to us now we're in Christ. God's grace doesn't end with salvation - that's just where it begins.

AS YOU HAVE RECEIVED

"As you therefore have received Christ Jesus the Lord, so walk in Him" (Colossians 2:6). The same way we entered into a relationship with God, is the same way we maintain our fellowship with God. How did you enter into this relationship with Him? "For by grace you have been saved through faith, and that not of yourselves; it is the gift of God, not of works, lest anyone should boast" (Ephesians 2:8-9). We put our faith in His grace and we were saved. Therefore, that's exactly how we should live the Christian life. The same principles of grace went into our receiving Christ should continue in our daily walk with Him.

Your being holy or your lack of holiness had nothing to do with God saving you, so why would it affect His blessing on your life now? Prior to your accepting Him, God didn't love you based on your "goodness," and now that you've accepted Him, His love is not withheld based on your poor performance. The same way we received Christ is the same way we must walk in Him: by grace through faith. There's nothing in the Bible that says you come to salvation through grace with a clean slate but after salvation have to start earning everything by "being good." It's become all too common for us to fall away from grace and focus more on our own works, which causes us to dwell on our performance rather than His promise. Once this happens, we start trying to earn from God rather than simply receiving what He's already given to us through grace.

FALLEN FROM GRACE

This is exactly what happened to the church in Galatia. If you aren't familiar with the Galatians, I'll recap: Paul and Barnabas started the Galatian church during one of their missionary journeys. Paul's routine was to get acquainted with the people of an area, evangelize, plant a church, train up leadership, and then head to the next city. After Paul and Barnabas planted the church in Galatia, a group of Christians, known as the Judaizers, came in and twisted the message of the gospel. When Paul heard how the gospel had been adulterated, he wrote to the Galatians: "I marvel that you are turning away so soon from Him who called you in the grace of Christ, to a different gospel, which is not another; but there are some who trouble you and want to pervert the gospel of Christ" (Galatians 1:6-7). Let's modernize Paul's message. He basically says, "Come on you guys, how have you already turned away from God and His grace? You're buying into this perverted gospel, but it's not even really a gospel. It doesn't compare to the good news

SAVED BY GRACE, BUT...

Jesus brings! You are listening to people who have completely distorted the message of the one true gospel." What false
reiteration of the gospel was Paul condemning? Essentially,
the Judaizers preached people were saved by grace but it was
their works that would make them righteous. They twisted the
original gospel from a grace-based faith into a works-based
religion.

Paul goes on to debunk the myth that good deeds and
earthly works can earn more of God's love and righteousness:
"O foolish Galatians! Who has bewitched you that you should
not obey the truth, before whose eyes Jesus Christ was clearly
portrayed among you as crucified? This alone I want to learn
from you: Did you receive the Spirit by the works of the law,
or by the hearing of faith? Are you so foolish? Having begun
in the Spirit, are you now being made perfect by the flesh?"
(Galatians 3:1-3).

The Galatians started out in grace and faith, but they allowed themselves to be led astray by the Judaizers. They
tossed their faith in God's grace aside and tried to earn favor and grow their relationships with the Lord by keeping
the works of the law. They were trying to become righteous
through their obedience to the rules. The Bible labels this type
of thinking as a "fall from grace." If after receiving Christ, you
continue to try to become more righteous and earn God's love
by performing works, then you've fallen away from grace. So
many of us have fallen victim to the same adulterated gospel

that fooled the Galatians. "You who are trying to be justified by law have been alienated from Christ; you have fallen away from grace" (Galatians 5:4).

So, Paul says those who try to justify themselves through works in order to gain Christ's love "have fallen away from grace." I used to believe a fall from grace applied to someone who received Christ but then went back to living by the ways of the world; someone who knew and accepted God's gospel, but returned to their sinful lifestyle. That's not even remotely close to what it means or what this verse is saying. In fact, it's basically the opposite. Someone who has fallen from grace is a person who has received Christ as their savior and is now trying to be made right with God through their own works. Grace is God's unearned, unmerited, favor and blessing, and when you try to merit what is unmerited, then you have fallen from grace. In essence, you've left the realm of grace and entered the realm of works.

There are so many Christians who have fallen from grace. They toil in order to gain God's love and approval through their own merit. They're trying to get God to move in their lives because of what they've done. It's interesting - you can tell by the way we pray for people that we don't really understand grace. We say things like "Oh God, please bless John. Lord, he has served You his whole life. He's been faithful to You all these years, and he loves You with all his heart." That's a prayer rooted in works. We're asking God to move in someone's life because of what they've done, not because of what Jesus did. I'm not saying any of this to make anyone feel bad or give anyone a guilt trip. The only reason I use this prayer as an example is because I've prayed that kind of prayer multiple times. God doesn't answer our prayers because of our years of faithful service. God answers our prayers because of the faithfulness of Jesus.

I talk with people all the time who are going through hardships, and they say things like, "I don't know why this happened to us. We go to church, tithe, pray, and feed the homeless. Why did this happen to us?" They understand salvation by grace, but they're living by works. They think because of their righteousness they shouldn't be experiencing certain difficulties. Look, it's great to be doing all of those things. Praying, tithing, giving to the needy - all of those things are great, but if you're doing them in order to get God to bless your life, then you've fallen from grace.

MANY TOIL IN ORDER TO GAIN GOD'S LOVE AND APPROVAL THROUGH THEIR OWN MERIT.

Let's look at what else the book of Galatians has to say about all of this. "[Therefore, I do not treat God's gracious gift as something of minor importance and defeat its very purpose]; I do not set aside and invalidate and frustrate and nullify the grace (unmerited favor) of God. For if justification (righteousness, acquittal from guilt) comes through [observing the ritual of] the Law, then Christ (the Messiah) died groundlessly and to no purpose and in vain. [His death was then wholly superfluous]" (Galatians 2:21 AMP). When you try to earn favor with God through performance, you *devalue* grace. On the other hand, if you feel you're unworthy of God's love and favor in your life because of your performance, then you too have fallen from grace. If you think you're disqualified from God's blessings or you're some sort of second-class citizen all because of some sin you committed, then you've fallen away from grace. To live in the grace zone and experience the power of God's grace in your life is to realize everything God gives us and does for us has nothing to do with our performance or lack thereof. It's based on the gift of grace. The same way we received Christ is the same way we continue to receive everything God has for us: by grace and through faith.

Jesus Christ has fulfilled every requirement for us to be loved, accepted, favored, and blessed. All that's left for us to do is rest in His finished work.

CHAPTER SEVEN

GET SOME REST

GET SOME REST

CHAPTER SEVEN

Sleep never comes easy for me. I could work all day, run a 5K, and then sprinkle Benadryl on my dinner, and I'd still have a tough time drifting off when my head finally hits a pillow. Certain key conditions need to be met before I can rest. First, the sleeping environment must be no warmer than 68 degrees Fahrenheit (this is not a game - Sixty. Eight. Degrees). Next, I need the steady drone of a humming fan to sing me to sleep. The perfect fan, of course, is in my bedroom at home. Unfortunately, I can't detach it from the ceiling and stow it in my carry-on bag when I travel, and not all hotels and guest rooms have fans with that soothing, monotonous mumble

I like. I do, however, own a travel fan that sings me to sleep when I'm on the road.

One time, I left my travel fan at home. In an insomnia-driven panic, I pulled out my phone and searched for a noise-producing app that might save me from a sleepless night. Now, it's no secret we live in the greatest time in the history the world: A time where humans can connect with other people from around the world through servers and wires; a time where we are literally learning how to print working arms and legs for people with injuries and deformities; a time where there should be a phone app designed to mimic soothing sounds for sleep-deprived people like me. As I thumbed my way through the app store, I came across a promising prospect: An app designed to produce soothing night-time noises. This particular app offered sounds of thunderstorms (which I chose not to use for fear of subconsciously peeing the bed), a cat purring (I'm more of a dog person), and even a series of chanting monks (nah, I'm good). But, alas - it offered no humming fans. Needless to say, my travel fan has not been left behind since that sleepless night.

On the rare occasion when the fan and the cool temperatures aren't doing the trick, I resort to my iPod. For whatever reason, my mind tends to be hyperactive at night, so it soothes me to listen to sermons while I go to sleep. And, when all else fails - melatonin. One of God's greatest gifts to mankind puts me right to bed. I also feel obligated to tell you, melatonin also works on children. Do with that information what you will.

In the same way certain conditions need to be met in order for me to get some shut-eye, so too, there are things that need to happen in order for us to rest in our relationship with God. Fortunately for us, Jesus Christ has fulfilled every requirement for us to be loved, accepted, favored, and blessed. All that's left for us to do is rest in His finished work. Thanks to Jesus, everything God has promised is ours through our faith and trust in Him. Hebrews chapter four expounds upon the rest we can experience:

> Therefore, since a promise remains of entering His rest, let us fear lest any of you seem to have come short of it. For indeed the gospel was preached to us as well as to them; but the word which they heard did not profit them, not being mixed with faith in those who heard it. For we who have believed do enter that rest, as He has said: "So I swore in My wrath, 'They shall not enter My rest,' " although the works were finished from the foundation of the world. (Hebrews 4:1-3).

These verses highlight a rest for the people of God. Israel entering into the Promised Land is a picture of God's promise of rest. Before Israel ever became a nation, God, through grace, provided a promise Israel would enter into this Promised Land. He promised Abraham 430 years earlier they would enter into that land (Genesis 15). God miraculously brought Israel out of the land of Egypt, through the desert, and into the Promised Land. If you're familiar with this story in Exodus, you might recall the Israelites didn't have the quickest, most direct journey from Egypt to the Promised Land. Their disbelief and rebellion kept them in the desert much longer than God wanted. They wandered around the desert for forty years because God's promise was met with doubt rather than faith. Everything we receive from God is always by grace through faith. *Everything.* By grace, God made a promise to them, but that promise didn't come to fruition for years because it wasn't met with faith. Grace alone is a one-sided affair in opposition to true love. We can only receive God's promises for us by combing grace and faith together. An entire generation missed out on the Promised Land because of their inability to believe.

For He has spoken in a certain place of the seventh day in this way: "And God rested on the seventh day from all His works"; and again in this place: "They shall not enter My rest." Since therefore it remains that some must enter it, and those to whom it was first preached did not enter because of disobedience, again He designates a certain day, saying in David, "Today," after such a long time, as it has been said: "Today, if you will hear His voice, Do not harden your hearts." For if Joshua had given them rest, then He would not afterward have spoken of another day.

(Hebrews 4:4-9).

If we break this verse down, we arrive at a rough translation that looks like this: "Don't be like the Israelites, who didn't receive rest due to their disbelief." The rest this verse talks about wasn't fulfilled when Joshua finally led the Israelites into the Promised Land because 400 years later David comes along and says, "There is a rest unto the people of God." Basically, the Promised Land the Israelites finally entered was but a mere picture of the rest God wanted to give. It was just a glimpse of the new covenant reality that offers us peace and security in Jesus Christ.

The rest these verses describe is not a physical rest. It goes all the way back to Genesis chapter two, where God rests on the seventh day of creation. While I'm sure creating a universe can be quite taxing, God didn't rest because He was worn out. He didn't need to take a sick day to catch up on some sleep. That's not the kind of rest God took. God's rest was an end to His creation. He simply ceased to create. His masterpiece was finished, complete, so He rested. It's like when an artist finishes a painting. When he sees the picture is perfect and there's nothing more to add, he rests. His work is complete. "Thus the heavens and the earth, and all the host of them, were finished. And on the seventh day God ended His work which was done, and He rested on the seventh day from all His work which He had done" (Genesis 2:1-2). God rested because His creation was complete.

God's creation was so perfect He didn't need to create any-thing else. "Then God said, 'Let the earth bring forth grass, the herb that yields seed, and the fruit tree that yields fruit accord-ing to its kind, whose seed is in itself, on the earth'; and it was so" (Genesis 1:11). When God created the trees, He created them with the seed to reproduce, so He would never have to create another tree. When God created the monkey, He creat-ed it with the ability to reproduce, so He would never have to make another monkey. The power to procreate is within the creation itself.

Thankfully, God didn't just give monkeys and other organ-isms the ability to procreate. We too were blessed with this ability. Thus, humanity presses on. Not only has our ability to procreate allowed our existence to continue, it has also pro-duced an endless supply of comedic conversations. Think about it: When a couple weds, one of the first questions peo-ple ask is, "When are you going to have kids?" After some good friends of mine got married, they responded to the question like this: "Well, we're just praying, and if God wants us to have kids, then we will. But, we won't have a child unless God wants us to." Their answer sounds nice, but I needed a little clarifica-tion. "So," I said, "you aren't using any kind of contraception?" "No," the husband replied, "it's in God's hands." I think some religious cliché compelled him to say this, but I had to tell him God was not in control of whether or not they had a baby. They were in control! They weren't using any sort of protection, which, the last time I checked, raises the chances of having a child by a pretty decent amount. God doesn't look down and say, "I'll give you a kid." God gave us the ability to reproduce, and unless you use protection (and sometimes even then) or you have a medical condition that prevents you from doing that, you will have a child. That's how God set it up to work. It didn't take long for my friends to discover this scientific fact. They had two children within the first two years of their marriage. God created things with the ability to reproduce, and then He rested because His creation was complete.

SABBATH

This day of rest God took became known as the Sabbath. Every week there is to be a Sabbath, a day of rest, when you stop working and cease creating in order to enjoy life. "So let no one judge you in food or in drink, or regarding a festival or a new moon or Sabbaths, which are a shadow of things to come, but the substance is of Christ" (Colossians 2:16-17). The Sabbath is only a shadow of something greater. The Sabbath is a shadow of the rest we as believers have in Christ.

In Genesis, God created man on the sixth day. He didn't create man on the first day and make him tread water until He created land. He didn't create man on the second day, when he'd have to wait an entire day before he could eat. God anticipated every need mankind would have before creating. Everything in creation was already complete before he created man. God made all of creation first. Then, at the very end, God created Adam and Eve. So when God entered into His rest on the seventh day, Adam and Eve also entered into that rest. There was nothing for them to do. There was nothing more to create, no work for them to get done. All they had to do was accept, rest, and enjoy.

The Sabbath foreshadows the rest we have in our relationship with God. The rest in Genesis is the rest of creation. Ours is the rest of redemption. In Jesus there is nothing left for you to do in order to be made right with God. There is nothing you have to do to gain God's acceptance. There are no hoops you need to jump through to merit God's love. All you have to do is rest and believe in the finished work of Jesus. "For in Him dwells all the fullness of the Godhead bodily; and you are complete in Him" (Colossians 2:10). In Jesus Christ you are complete. You don't need to add anything else to what He did. It's finished. The only thing you need to do is cease from your own works.

> **THE REST IN GENESIS IS THE REST OF CREATION, OURS IS THE REST OF REDEMPTION.**

"For he who has entered His rest has himself also ceased from his works as God did from His" (Hebrews 4:10). In order to enter into this rest, you have to cease from your own works. You have to stop trying to be accepted by God. You have to cease trying to earn God's favor. You have to forget about earning His love through your performance and simply accept the fact He has already done everything for you. When entering into His rest, you can't look to anything other than the cross to receive His blessing. We must stop striving for His love, stop trying to earn what's been freely given, and learn to rest in the completed work of His grace.

Rest in the fact there's nothing left for you to do. The work of Jesus on the cross is complete, therefore all you have to do is believe. Once you believe, then you can enter into the same rest Adam and Eve were born into at the beginning of creation: No work, no assignment, no striving - God did everything for us through Christ. Accept what God's grace has already provided. The Christian life is all about His grace from beginning to end.

LABOR

"Let us labor therefore to enter into that rest" (Hebrews 4:11). That kind of sounds like an oxymoron, right? How in the world do you labor *and* rest? It actually takes a lot of effort to enter into God's rest because we've been raised in a world where we get what we deserve. We've been conditioned to think in a way that doesn't always align with God's grace. We're taught nothing in life is free. If you want something, you've got to earn it. The ideals of our world are contrary to grace. You, like me, are going to have to work to enter into God's

YOU HAVE TO CONSTANTLY REMIND YOURSELF WHAT GOD HAS ALREADY ACCOMPLISHED ON YOUR BEHALF IN ORDER TO REMAIN IN THE GRACE ZONE.

grace-given rest. We have to work past all sorts of contradictory messages that come at us from society, churches, other Christians, and even our own minds. These things try to pull us away from God's grace and into a works-based faith. The labor this verse is talking about includes combating thoughts like, "God can't bless you now because of what you've done; you're such a hypocrite; you've been saved for all these years, yet you still struggle with this-or-that; don't expect God to answer your prayers now." These thoughts do not line up with who God is and take a lot of energy and effort to keep at bay.

You're going to have to labor to enter into the rest God promises. It's going to take effort. You have to constantly remind yourself what God has already accomplished on your behalf in order to remain in the grace zone. It's not something that happens instantly. It doesn't happen just because you hear a message on grace or read a book on grace. Just when I think I've got the grace thing figured out, I find myself slipping back into my old ways of thinking. It's a constant labor to believe God's love and acceptance of me has nothing to do with my performance, but the labor is worth the rest that's waiting for us. So, let's all get some rest?

The law cannot clean us nor can it make us righteous. It can only show us how unrighteous we are so that we might turn to The One who can wash us white as snow.

FREE FROM LAW

FREE FROM LAW

CHAPTER EIGHT

At our church we celebrate the holiday season in the tradition of our forefathers and their mothers and fathers before them. As soon as the seasonal lights start to flicker, the Christmas trees dance with decorations, the racially inaccurate nativity scenes start to populate countless yards and the church staff gathers to enjoy a traditional evening of "Dirty Santa." Yes - you read that correctly - "Dirty Santa." I know what you're thinking: "What an odd game for a church staff to play." But if you've ever played, then you know just how great this game can be. In case you haven't had the opportunity to get heated for the holidays with a round of "Dirty Santa," the rules are as follows: Each individual brings in a gift, and worth around ten dollars. Once everyone arrives with his or her gift, we draw numbers to determine the order in which players can choose gifts. Once it's your turn, you have the option to steal someone's unwrapped gift or to choose from the pile of remaining wrapped presents.

One year, a staff member bought some scratch-off lottery tickets. He wrapped them in a very unassuming manor and placed them on the gifts table. As the game progressed, his wife actually ended up with the lottery tickets. As the game came to an end, she was still holding the unscratched tickets. Curious to see if she was a winner, everyone gathered around to watch her scratch the numbers. She etched away at the silver coating, advancing down the line of potential winning combinations. As she scratched, a winner was revealed! She scratched away at the prize to see she'd won the grand prize - $10,000! Her eyes glowed with excitement and she instantly began to talk about how she planned to spend the money. As she listed the things she wanted to purchase, her eyes met her husband's. An irrepressible smirk spread across his face, and she knew it was too good to be true. The tickets were phony. They were fake winners, designed to crush the spirit they had just lifted. Everyone but her burst into laughter as she let the false tickets fall to the ground. It wasn't good news for her, but it was the best news for him.

Good news for one person isn't always good news for others. When God initially started to unfold the gospel of grace to me, I understood for the first time why the gospel is referred to as "the good news." In these early moments of excitement, my optimism led me to believe everyone would be as happy as I was to hear about the revelation of the gospel of grace. I thought good news would be just that: good for everyone. I mean, come on, who doesn't like hearing good news about themselves? Apparently, a lot of people. I soon discovered many Christians have grown so accustomed to hearing bad news that when they hear the good news, it can be startling.

Our church has a reputation for being a place of grace. While I think this is the best kind of reputation, locals often ask me if my church is "one of those feel-good churches?" My response is always the same: "Is your church a feel-bad church?" Look, the Bible says the gospel is good news. In my experience with good news, it usually makes you feel good. Therefore, the gospel should make you feel great because it is literally the best news! Unfortunately, I soon realized not everyone who came to our church left feeling good, much less great. The Gospel is only good to those who know and accept their need for grace. The same graceful news that is good for one person can be downright offensive for someone relegated to the rules of religion. If you're self-righteous, unloving, and judgmental, then the gospel of grace isn't good news to you.

THE SAME GRACEFUL NEWS THAT IS GOOD FOR ONE PERSON CAN BE DOWNRIGHT OFFENSIVE FOR SOMEONE RELEGATED TO THE RULES OF RELIGION.

That's why Jesus offended the religious leaders with His message while sinners drew near to Him. Those who don't think they need saving aren't as apt to listen and accept the good news. It's no different today. Grace still offends the religious. That's why there are so many messages trying to deface grace. They blame the sin problem in the church on "greasy grace." They chalk lukewarm Christianity in America up to "sloppy agape." And, no, I did not make these phrases up. These are actual slogans I've heard and seen pastors use in a misguided attempt to belittle the message of grace. They say things like, "We don't need more feel-good messages about grace. We need people who will stand up and preach against sin."

I don't think the message of grace is the problem with the church in America because the vast majority of Christians have never even heard the pure undiluted message of grace, but I'm almost certain they've heard plenty of messages preaching against sin.

I worked with teenagers for years, and if you ask the average teenager what it means to be a Christian, they'll start to list all the sins you shouldn't commit. I believe people have heard enough of the rule-based Christianity. That message, far more than the message of grace, has been overused and proved ineffective. The hard-line message against sin hasn't curbed humanity's issues with sin one bit.

Once again, don't get me wrong. I believe in holiness and

living a righteous lifestyle. I just don't believe telling people what the rules are and reminding them time and time again they've broken them produces authentic holiness. Laying down the law every Sunday hasn't produced obedience. In fact, this tends to produce the opposite. Preaching the law (the Ten Commandments) actually causes more sin. I know it sounds crazy, but that's what the Bible says: "moreover the law entered that the offense (sin) might abound. But where sin abounded, grace abounded much more" (Romans 5:20). The law was never given as guidelines to make you holy. The purpose of the law was to reveal sin, to shed light on how sinful we are, so we would see our need for a savior. It's written throughout the New Testament:

> For no one can ever be made right with God by doing what the law commands. The law simply shows us how sinful we are. (Romans 3:20)

> What shall we say then? Is the law sin? Certainly not! On the contrary, I would not have known sin except through the law. (Romans 7:7)

> The law was our tutor to bring us to Christ. (Galatians 3:24).

The purpose of the law is to drive us to Christ. Once you've received Christ, the law's job is done. It fulfilled its purpose. I'm not advocating lawlessness. Yet, put simply, the law is unnecessary in the life of the believer.

> *But we know that the law is good if one uses it lawfully, knowing this: that the law is not made for a righteous person, but for the lawless and insubordinate, for the ungodly and for sinners, for the unholy and profane, for murderers of fathers and murderers of mothers, for manslayers, for fornicators, for sodomites, for kidnappers, for liars, for perjurers, and if there is any other thing that is contrary to sound doctrine. (1 Timothy 1:8-10)*

The law itself isn't inherently evil or bad. It's good when used properly. One time, when I was about 10 years old, a friend of mine was trying to use his dad's pressure washer. Being about the same age as I was, this kid didn't know how to use a pressure washer any more than I did. So, he did what any logical, average 10-year-old boy would do. He pointed the pressure washer at his hand and pulled the trigger. The blade of water sliced his skin, leaving an open gash behind. I think we can all agree the pressure washer wasn't evil. This machine wasn't out to get my friend. He just didn't know how to properly use it, resulting in his own injury and what could have been injury to others. The same goes for the law. If used for its intended purpose, the law is good. Its proper use is not for the righteous, but for those who have not received Je-

THE LAW IS INTENDED TO REVEAL THE SIN IN OUR LIVES AND SHOW US OUR NEED OF A SAVIOR. sus. It's intended to reveal the sin in our lives and show us our need of a Savior. I love how the Amplified Bible reflects this sentiment in Romans 5:20: "But then law came in, [only] to expand and increase the trespass [making it more apparent and exciting opposition]." Not only does the law expand and increase sin, but it also makes you want to break it!

PRINCIPLE OF LAW

I don't know about you, but every time I walk past a sign that says, "Do Not Touch", it makes me want to run my hand across it. I never intended to touch the wall in the first place, but now that you told me not to, I'm about to lay hands on this thing. Don't even get me started on, "Wet Paint Do Not Touch." Now they've really gotten my rebellious heart's attention. Immediately, my mind starts to wander. "Is it really wet?" I ask myself. "I wonder how long that sign has been up? I bet the paint is probably dry by now," I say as I run my hands along the forbidden façade. I know exactly what will happen if the paint isn't dry, but being instructed not to do something stirs up a desire to do just that. It's human nature to do what we're told not to do.

I once heard a story about a museum that had this particular antique desk on display. The desk was so old the dirt and oils covering our hands could prove harmful to the integrity of the antique, so the museum put a "Do Not Touch" sign on the desk. Despite their attempts to stop people from touching the piece, it was covered in fingerprints every day. While the exhibit director wanted guests to be able to get a close, personal look at the antique, he couldn't bear the thought of the desk being ruined. So instead of encasing the piece or establishing a rope barrier, the museum director put a new sign on the desk reading, "Please wash hands after touching the exhibit." After the new sign was erected, the exhibit director reported the number of people touching the piece dropped drastically. The "Do Not Touch" sign made people want to touch it even more.

When I first had the opportunity to share this very human desire to do the opposite of what we're told, I wanted to illustrate the subject. Our church has a unique layout requiring guests to walk down a long hallway in order to get to the sanctuary. Prior to our remodel the front doors opened to reveal this hallway that we referred to as the "green mile," partly because of its length, and partly because of its tragic, green carpet color. Along the green mile, there are two different doors opening directly to the sanctuary. The first door you encounter upon entering the building contains a small window. No one uses this door, besides the worship team because it spits you out directly in front of the stage for all to see. To get to the other door that opens more inconspicuously toward the back of the sanctuary, you must brave the green mile gauntlet, nodding pleasantly, hugging necks, and dodging hands holding hot coffee all along the way.

One Sunday morning I put a sign on the window of the first door reading, "Do not look through window." I stood in the hallway across from the first door and watched as people started pouring into the building. Most people immediately noticed the sign and questioned why they weren't allowed to look through the window. After receiving a vague, unsatisfactory answer, many of those people would go and peer through the window despite the ominous sign. One person remarked, "I walk by that window every single week, and I never once wanted to look through it until now." The moment I put that sign up it made everyone want to look through the window. That's what the law does. It makes sin more apparent, more visible. It draws our attention to it and stirs up a desire within us to either break the rules or break free from them.

STRENGTH OF SIN

First Corinthians 15:56 states "the sin's strength is the law." Did you get that? All of sin's power comes from the law. Here's a metaphor to help me visualize Christianity in regards to the law. I work out occasionally - not enough to make much of a difference, but one of my favorite things to do is bench press. Bench-pressing the bar by itself is easy enough. It only weighs 45 pounds. Benching the bar requires minimal effort. Therefore, I add some weight. The weight provides the necessary resistance which pushes me to work harder. As the weight increases, so does the level of difficulty. The weight increases as my reps decrease until I'm no longer able to lift the bar at all. I'll spare you the details on how much I can actually lift. It's far too embarrassing.

Our Christian walk should be as natural and doable as lifting that bar. Every law is like adding more weight onto the bar: the more laws placed upon you, the heavier the bar becomes, until you just can't lift all of the weight anymore and the bar comes crashing down on your chest. "The strength of sin is the law." Sin is empowered in our lives when we live under the weight of the law. The very rules we place upon people in order to get them to live holy are tragically at the root of their defeat. The person who focuses on keeping rules will experience constant frustration and failure because it's impossible to lift all that weight.

When your Christian life is made up of a bunch of do's and don'ts, it just doesn't work. Have you ever tried to go on a diet and failed? I have. Plenty of times. Then I move on to a different diet and fail again. I don't know about you, but anytime I've attempted a diet, all I can think about are the select foods I'm not supposed to eat. Tell me I can't eat sweets and my mind won't stop thinking about treats until my sweet tooth is saturated with sugar. It's just the way we're wired. Self-control is an admirable and necessary characteristic to possess, but even the most controlled people will eventually fail if the law is continuously tossed in their faces and held over their heads.

The same thing can happen in our relationships with God. The moment you resolve to start reading your Bible and praying for at least thirty minutes, you turn those actions into laws. **THE MOMENT YOU IMPOSE RULES UPON A RELATIONSHIP IT BECOMES MORE ABOUT OBLIGATION THAN DESIRE.** After a few days or weeks in a ritualistic relationship with Christ, the last thing you want to do is devote those thirty minutes to this required routine you've imposed upon yourself. But since you committed, you drag yourself out of bed to pray and read Scripture. I've been there. I've been the guy who resolved to devote thirty minutes to prayer and prayed my heart out only to realize that a measly five minutes had passed. The moment you impose rules upon a relationship it becomes more about obligation than desire. Placing a "thou shalt" on something can drain the life out of even the most enjoyable events.

MINISTRY OF DEATH

When you bring the law into your relationship with God, it only produces death. Take a look at what Paul's letter to the Corinthians had to say about the law in regards to a relationship with Christ. "Not that we are sufficient of ourselves to think of anything as being from ourselves, but our sufficiency is from God, who also made us sufficient as ministers of the new covenant, not of the letter but of the Spirit; for the letter kills, but the Spirit gives life" (2 Corinthians 3:5-6).

We are no longer under the ministry of the Old Covenant, which was the covenant of law. We've been given a New Covenant, a covenant of grace! The phrase, "the letter kills" refers to the law in this passage. You've probably heard of "the letter of the law," right? When you bring the law into any area of your life, it is destined to bring death and despair.

While the letter of the law promises death, the word of the spirit offers life. In Exodus, when Moses returned from the mountain top where God gave him the Ten Commandments, the people at the base of the mountain were worshipping a golden calf. Seeing the people, Moses said, "Whoever is on God's side come over here and everyone else over there." After separating the people, those who chose the golden calf over the Lord were killed. The Bible says "about 3,000 died that day" (Exodus 32:28). So, when the law first came down from the mount, it brought with it the death of 3,000 people. Thankfully, there's a redemptive end to this story. You see, on the day of Pentecost, over 120 people gathered in the upper room. In this upper room, the Holy Spirit was poured out. Inspired by the spirit, Peter got up and preached. The Bible goes on to say, "about 3,000 were saved" (Acts 2:41). At the coming of the law "about 3,000 died," and at the coming of the Spirit "about 3,000 were saved." The letter kills but the Spirit gives life.

But if the ministry of death, written and engraved on stones, was glorious, so that the children of Israel could not look steadily at the face of Moses because of the glory of his countenance, which glory was passing away, how will the ministry of the Spirit not be more glorious? For, if the ministry of condemnation had glory, the ministry of righteousness exceeds much more in glory. (2 Corinthians 3:7-9)

Here, the Bible calls the law "the ministry of death" and "condemnation." The more laws you impose upon your life, or allow others to place upon you, the more death and condemnation you'll have in your life. This verse makes it so clear. And, just in case you might have thought the scriptures about the law refer to the ceremonial law and not the Ten Commandments, this verse references the law as "the ministry of death, written and engraved on stones." The ceremonial law wasn't written on stone - the Ten Commandments were engraved on stone.

I'm not against the law. It's an expression of the holiness of God. It reveals God's righteous standards, and it sheds light on our sin. The law is necessary. But imagine this for a moment: Let's say you wake up in the morning and look in the mirror to discover you have visible grease streaked across your face. What's the logical thing to do? Take the mirror off the wall and try to clean your face with the mirror? While the mirror reveals the grease, it's not helpful in the actual act of cleaning.

The mirror, like the law, is simply there to show us we have something needing to be cleaned and taken care of. The law reveals our dirtiness, but it's usefulness ends there. Just as the mirror is only helpful in revealing the dirt, but not actually removing it, so too the law is helpful in highlighting our sin but not actually helping us move past it. Where the mirror's usefulness ends, soap and water's usefulness begins. In the same way, where the law's influence ends, the spirit's begins. After the law points out the problem, God's grace takes over. Don't attempt to use the law to wash your sins away. That's what the Holy Spirit and the promise of grace are for! When we look into the perfect standard of God's righteousness, we'll inevitably see how dirty we are. The law cannot clean us nor can it make us righteous. It can only show us how unrighteous we are so we might turn to The One who can wash us white as snow.

Where the Old Covenant based its blessings on earned favor through adherence to the law, the New Covenant does just the opposite.

NEW OPERATING SYSTEM

NEW OPERATING SYSTEM

CHAPTER NINE

I tend to take things a little too far at times. You've probably gathered this much from the strange stories I've recount-
ed thus far. I remember one time when some of the students
from our youth ministry tried to mess with my wife and me
by dumping an old Christmas tree on our front porch. You're
probably thinking, "what a lame prank," and I couldn't agree
more. Incredibly lame. So lame, in fact, someone needed to
teach them a lesson in pranking. Upon hearing them outside,
I sprang into action. I grabbed my fully loaded paintball gun,
(because who doesn't have a fully loaded, ready-to-go paintball gun handy?) and proceeded to burst through my front

door. The unsuspecting pranksters made a break for it, diving into their getaway car. As they threw the car into gear, I did my best "Mission Impossible" impersonation and leapt onto the roof of their moving vehicle. You see, their first mistake was attempting a lame prank on me. Their second mistake was leaving the sunroof open. I stuck the barrel of the paintball gun through the roof of their car and began to fire a barrage of blind shots at the perpetrators. It was at this point I realized all of these pranksters were girls. I could still argue my actions were justified, but in hindsight, I might've taken my retaliation a little too far. It was still by far the closest I'll ever be to James Bond.

Like most men, the one person who has to deal with my excessive retaliation more than anyone is my wife, Brynn. We tend to mess around a lot when we're home, joking with one another or pulling pranks. But what starts as innocent fun often gets out of hand. One time, she put an ice cube down the back of my shirt. Innocent enough, right? My response was to dump a large glass of ice water on top of her head. I saw no other way to even the score. Drastic times call for drastically cold measures. After this type of response, she often looks at me, like most normal people would, with an expression of sheer shock. My justification is always the same: "You started it!" Usually, we jibe back and forth about the events that led us to where we are now, but whether she's sopping wet, buried underneath a pillow fort, or pinned to the floor, the battle always ends the moment that first tear starts to surface on her face.

The second I see a tear glistening in her eyes, I'm a beaten man. It's over. She wins. I lose. It no longer matters who started it or if my actions were "justified." When I see I've actually hurt her, the profuse apologies begin. I immediately feel the need to make amends. I value our relationship so much I can't stand it when things aren't right between us. That's the difference between living under law and living under grace. When living under law, obedience is about keeping the rules. But, when we're living under grace, obedience is all about valuing our relationship with God. When you value something, it doesn't feel like a set of rigid restrictions you have to follow. Your heart becomes naturally submissive in a relationship you value. That's the power of grace: grace transcends the law.

But, I've discovered many Christians aren't living under pure law or pure grace. Instead they are living with a mixture of both law and grace. They mix a little bit of the Old Covenant with a little bit of the New Covenant. The problem is when you mix grace with anything else, then it's no longer grace. This is what Galatians means when it says, "a little leaven leavens the whole lump" (Galatians 5:9). This verse isn't talking about sin, it's talking about the law. When you mix the law with grace, it creates something totally separate from the grace God intended.

WHEN YOU MIX THE LAW WITH GRACE IT CREATES SOMETHING TOTALLY SEPARATE FROM THE GRACE THAT GOD INTENDED.

Growing up in Las Vegas made me a buffet expert. The easiest way to separate the weak sauce from the buffet ballers is to judge the person's line speed. Rookies tend to walk through the smörgåsbord at a sluggish pace, inspecting each item on every platter. But the experts, like myself, have mastered the art of the buffet. We glide through the line with an ease that only comes from years of buffeting. Rookies carefully choose what they want to put on their plate, but experts just throw it on their plate and then decide if they want to eat it later. (Lord, forgive me for the gluttonous glories of my buffet habits).

Now that we're nice and hungry, allow me to tie all of this together. I feel like we've all, at one time or another, treated the two covenants like a buffet. We take a little bit of New Covenant grace and little Old Covenant law. We take the parts we like from each covenant and leave the parts we don't like. We pick parts of the law we find easiest to follow, while leaving the hard parts behind. The problem is this "buffet mentality" creates a deadly mixture of the two covenants which spoils God's grace.

DIFFERENT OPERATING SYSTEMS

The covenant of law and the covenant of grace operate on two completely different systems. Trying to mix them is like taking a new Macbook and attempting to run Windows' first operating system, MS-DOS. That old software won't work on the new computer; it has a completely different system for operations. The same goes for your walk with Christ: if you are in the New Covenant and you are trying to pattern your life based on the Old Covenant principles, then it's not going to work because they are complete opposites. You can't take a little out of the Old and mix it with a little bit of the New because the two don't mix.

If you want proof these two covenants are separate and not meant for mixing, then take a look at this: Under the Old Covenant, God says, "I will by no means clear the guilty, but I will visit their sins to the third and fourth generations" (Exodus 34:7). Okay, that's a pretty tough grudge to overcome. But, under the New Covenant God says, "I will be merciful to their unrighteousness and their sins, and their lawless deeds I will remember no more" (Hebrews 8:12). The two covenants run in opposition to each other, yet you have Christians with one foot in the Old Covenant and one foot in the New Covenant. They are trying to live in both. They believe they have to keep all the rules to be blessed and that grace is for the times they mess up. We have Christians who think we need to keep the law, and the parts of the law we fail to keep, grace takes care of.

In Mark chapter two, Jesus gives us a metaphor for the two covenants: "and no one puts new wine into old wineskins; or else the new wine bursts the wineskins, the wine is spilled, and the wineskins are ruined. But new wine must be put into new wineskins" (Mark 2:22). The new wine represents the covenant of grace, while the old wineskin represents the law. If you've ever seen an old wineskin, then you know they're firm and inflexible. That's the law. It's stiff. It's not malleable in the least. The old wineskin wasn't designed for the new wine, so it bursts, spilling and ruining both the wine and the container. When you pour the new wine of grace into the old wineskin, you lose both. When you taint grace with the law, then you limit God's free and unmerited favor. Look at what Galatians has to say on the matter: "I do not nullify the grace of God, for if righteousness comes through the Law, then Christ died needlessly" (Galatians 2:21 NASB).

If you try to mix law and grace, you nullify the grace of God. "God resists the proud, but gives grace to the humble" (James 4:6). The proud are self-righteous people who trust in their own works to make them right with God. If we could've made ourselves right with God, then He wouldn't have sent His only son as a sacrifice to save us. God's grace doesn't operate in the lives of those who are living under law. It only works for those who are humble, those who know there's nothing they can do to earn right standing with God. Those people receive God's abundant grace. Recognizing your standing with God is based on grace alone is what qualifies you to receive more grace. What a brilliantly designed system!

"In that He says, 'A new covenant,' He has made the first obsolete. Now what is becoming obsolete and growing old is ready to vanish away" (Hebrews 8:13). The Old Covenant is now obsolete. It's out of date. It's old software that's no longer useful. If the Old Covenant is a Zune, then the New Covenant is the iPod—actually even better than the iPod. It's the Apple product that never goes out of style and will never need updating. While The Bible says the Old Covenant is vanishing away, there will always be religious teachers who try to bring it back to life. There will always be the temptation to return to a works-based faith and righteousness.

Galatians 5:1 provides some encouraging words on the issue: "stand fast therefore in the liberty by which Christ has made us free, and do not be entangled again with a yoke of bondage." When I'd hear people use this verse in sermons, they'd always talk about not getting entangled or trapped in sin. It was only when I realized the entire book of Galatians talks about the faulty system of mixing the law with grace that I finally understood what this verse is actually saying: The yoke of bondage refers to the law. Christ has set us free from the law and all its requirements. It's a verse of encouragement, not warning! If we were trying to translate the verse into layman's terms, it might sound something like this: "Now that you've been set free, don't revert back to the law. Don't be bound by works. Live in Christ's grace and the freely given, totally unmerited favor He offers. Stand fast in the gospel of grace and rest in Christ's finished work."

OLD COVENANT

In the Old Covenant, God deals with man through the lens of the law. Before the New Covenant came, people had to earn God's blessing and favor by adhering to the law. This legal relationship is apparent in Exodus 20 when God gives the Ten Commandments to Moses. Inscribed on the tablets were a bunch of dos and don'ts. It was literally a list of laws they had to keep in order to remain right with God. Deuteronomy 28 reinforces the legal relationship that existed before the New Covenant by listing all the conditional blessings of the Old Covenant. Everything here is dependent upon obedience to the law. "Now it shall come to pass, if you diligently obey the voice of the Lord your God, to observe carefully all His commandments which I command you today, that the Lord your God will set you high above all nations of the earth. And all these blessings shall come upon you and overtake you because you obey the voice of the Lord your God" (Deuteronomy 28:1-2; 14).

This passage goes on to list all the blessings available if one observes all of God's commandments. And, just in case you missed it, verse fourteen sums everything up by reiterating the fact that perfect obedience is required to walk in the blessings of God. Perfect obedience. That means ALL of the commandments must be kept at ALL times in order to receive God's blessings and walk in His favor. Deuteronomy doesn't play around—it goes on to list all the curses that can, and will, come upon you if you don't perfectly obey God's commandments. The list of curses spans from verse fifteen all the way to verse sixty-eight. That's a lot of curses; fifty-three verses worth, to be exact. The Old Covenant required complete obedience. In the rest of the Old Testament, we see this covenant being worked out in the lives of the Israelites. There were short periods where they obeyed God and were blessed, but most of the time they were disobedient. During those times of disobedience, we see the curses of Deuteronomy 28 carried out in the Israelites' lives. Believe it or not, it's hard to be perfect. The entire basis of the Old Covenant was to do right in order to avoid curses and receive blessings. The Old Covenant was rooted in law and fully dependent upon man's obedience. It's a covenant of deserved favor and blessing earned through righteous behavior and adherence to a set of guidelines. Thankfully for us, God gave us a New Covenant.

NEW COVENANT

For if that first covenant had been faultless, then no place would have been sought for a second. But finding fault with them, The Lord says: "Behold, the days are coming when I will make a New Covenant with the house of Israel and with the house of Judah— not according to the covenant that I made with their fathers in the days when I took them by

the hand to lead them out of the land of Egypt; because they did not continue in My covenant, and I disregarded them. For this is the covenant that I will make with the house of Israel now: I will put My laws in their mind and write them on their hearts; and I will be their God, and they shall be My people. None of them shall teach his neighbor, and none his brother, saying, 'Know the Lord,' for all shall know Me, from the least of them to the greatest of them. For I will be merciful to their unrighteousness, and their sins and their lawless deeds I will remember no more."
(Hebrews 8:7-12)

God found fault with the Old Covenant, so He made a New Covenant. The reason God found fault with the Old Covenant wasn't because there was anything wrong with the law. The problem was the Old Covenant was dependent upon our obedience. We were the problem with the first covenant. So, in the New Covenant, God removed us from the equation. The New Covenant is between God The Father and God The Son. It has nothing to do with us or our obedience, but everything to do with the faithfulness of Jesus.

Jesus is the mediator for the New Covenant (Hebrews 8:6; 9:15; 12:24). In the original Greek the word *mediator* translates as "a go between."[7] It's someone who goes between two parties and brings them together. Jesus Christ became a man so He could create the New Covenant and bring us to God. All we need to do to enter into the New Covenant is to realize and accept what Jesus did for us on the cross. It's important for us to understand the New Covenant is not dependent upon our adherence to the law. That was the old way, and this is the new. This New Covenant is purely based on Jesus. That means it's out of our hands. We couldn't break the New Covenant if we tried. That's why the New Covenant doesn't contain any of those old curses for breaking it. You can't break it because you didn't make it. And, since you can't break it, any and all curses are nullified, leaving only the blessings. The New Covenant is a covenant of grace. It's a covenant of undeserved favor and blessing that defies human logic. Where the Old Covenant based its blessings on earned favor through adherence to the law, the New Covenant does just the opposite. We no longer have to live perfectly by the law in order to be blessed and walk in God's favor. In the New Covenant, all of God's blessings come to us by grace, which means they're freely given. No amount of rule keeping or law abiding can earn what is already freely offered. The New Covenant is faultless because it's not based on anything we do. It's based solely on Christ's perfect obedience, which was, is, and will forever be without fault.

LAW FULFILLED

Jesus came as a man to fulfill every requirement of the law on our behalf. "Do not think that I came to destroy the Law or the Prophets. I did not come to destroy but to fulfill" (Matthew 5:17). All we were unable to do, He did on our behalf. Where we failed to wholly observe the law, Jesus succeeded. He didn't come for Himself; He came to fulfill the law *for us* so that *through Him* we could be credited with fulfilling the law. We literally couldn't keep the law, so He came and did it for us. I remember the specific moment when God spoke to me about this. I was reading about all of those blessings and curses in Deuteronomy when it hit me, "there's no way I'll ever get any of these blessings. I've broken these commandments time and time again." Before I could even finish my thought, I heard God speak to me. He assured me, "Jesus perfectly obeyed all the commandments. He has qualified you to receive all the blessings of the covenant." Where I failed to obey the commandments, Jesus succeeded on my behalf. How awesome is that? In that moment, God eased all of my self-doubt and fear by reassuring me Jesus did the job I never could.

JESUS DIDN'T COME FOR HIMSELF; HE CAME TO FULFILL THE LAW FOR US SO THAT THROUGH HIM WE COULD BE CREDITED WITH FULFILLING THE LAW.

Imagine running a marathon, but within the first mile of the race, you roll your ankle and can't go on. They take you to the medical tent, patch you up as best they can, and let you sit near the finish line. A couple of hours later you see one of the well-trained and conditioned Kenyans round the corner. No one is even close to him as he sprints across the finish line for his first-place finish. Cameras flash and fans erupt in applause, but when they try to place the first-place medal around his neck, he takes it from them and gives it to you. Not only does the winner decide to give you the trophy for winning first place, but he also gives you the $200,000 prize money. You received all the benefits of running and *winning* the marathon, even though you didn't make it past the first mile. That's what Jesus did for us: He ran the race we couldn't complete. We were disqualified before things even got going, but He perfectly followed all of the commandments on our behalf. God uses grace to transfer Jesus' perfect track record to us. He did all of the work and we reap all the rewards. That is grace!

It's impossible to receive the blessings God's grace promises if we don't buy in to what He says about us.

CHAPTER TEN

GRASS-HOPPER THINKING

GRASSHOPPER THINKING

CHAPTER TEN

One time, I was at the movies with my wife, washing buttered popcorn down with gulps of soda, when nature called. I don't usually like to get up to use the restroom mid-movie, but the giant drink I'd just absent-mindedly downed made it unavoidable. I tiptoed down the aisle, rushed out the door, and raced into the bathroom, determined not to miss much of the movie. Once in the stall, I heard a few people enter the bathroom. As they carried on their conversation, my heart sank. These were female voices. Yep, I was in the ladies' room.

Panic set in as I began planning my escape. I realized the air vents were out of reach and I wasn't James Bond, so there was only one way out. I had to keep the stall locked, wait until these ladies left, and then make a swift exit. As I patiently waited for the last of the women to leave, I braced myself for the getaway. That's when disaster struck. In what I can only assume was the mass exodus of every movie in the theater, women began piling into the restroom in droves. The lines lengthened, and soon the sea of people stretched out of the doors and down the hallway. I had no choice. I gathered myself, lowered my head, and walked out of that stall as fast as I could. I was greeted by what felt like thousands of women. Many of them were shocked, but their shock quickly became anger as they hurled expletives at the creeper in the women's restroom. I escaped with my life, but a small piece of my dignity still remains in that restroom. While this embarrassing identity crisis was a result of carelessness, things can get extremely messy when you don't understand who you are.

In Numbers 13, the Israelites came down with a case of mistaken identity. They didn't see themselves the way God saw them. They couldn't even see themselves the way surrounding nations saw them, which led to some very profound problems. Take a look at what happened after Moses sent spies to investigate the Land of Milk and Honey:

> Now they departed and came back to Moses and
> Aaron and all the congregation of the children of
> Israel in the Wilderness of Paran, at Kadesh; they
> brought back word to them and to all the congre-

gation, and showed them the fruit of the land. Then they told him: "We went to the land where you sent us. It truly flows with milk and honey, and this is its fruit. Nevertheless the people who dwell in the land are strong; the cities are fortified and very large; moreover we saw the descendants of Anak there. The Amalekites dwell in the land of the South; the Hittites, the Jebusites, and the Amorites dwell in the mountains; and the Canaanites dwell by the sea and along the banks of the Jordan." Then Caleb quieted the people before Moses, and said, "Let us go up at once and take possession, for we are well able to overcome it." But the men who had gone up with him said, "We are not able to go up against the people, for they are stronger than we." And they gave the children of Israel a bad report of the land which they had spied out, saying, "The land through which we have gone as spies is a land that devours its inhabitants, and all the people whom we saw in it are men of great stature. There we saw the giants (the descendants of Anak came from the giants); and we were like grasshoppers in our own sight, and so we were in their sight." (Numbers 13:26-33).

A quick recap so we can see the whole picture here: Moses sends out 12 of his best leaders on a spying mission. For forty days they scope out the scene. They get the lay of the land. They determine this place truly is the land promised to them by God. It's just as He described it, "a land flowing with milk and honey." After trekking through the wilderness, there's finally a light at the end of the tunnel. They found an oasis at the end of the desert. The Bible says there were grapes so large they had to carry them back on a pole supported by two people. I don't care how many giants inhabited that land, they had me at gargantuan grapes and a promise from God. So, Israel was on the cusp of entering into the Promised Land. God guaranteed victory, but out of twelve spies, only two came back confident the Israelites could take this land. This should never have been an investigation into whether it could be done, for God told the Israelites they *would* be the ones to do it. This should have been a recon mission designed to develop the best plan of attack, but these guys came back complaining there was no way to take the land because its inhabitants were strong, the cities were fortified, and the giants were, well, *giant*. The only people who brought back promising reports were Joshua and Caleb. Ten out of twelve spies failed to recognize their assured identity in God. It was because of Israel's unbelief that they failed to enter the Promised Land and were forced to wander the wilderness for forty more years.

Events such as this one in the Old Testament can provide a picture of the Christian life. Just as Israel was assured the Promised Land, we too have been granted an inheritance. God has a destiny and a purpose for all of our lives. Using the Israelites as an example, we should be able to determine what's keeping us from walking in God's purpose for our lives. If we are promised a land of milk and honey, then what's keeping us in the desert? For the Israelites, it was self-doubt. It was a lack of confidence in the identity God spoke over their lives that kept them from immediately entering the Promised Land. The same sort of doubt threatens to keep us walking in God's purpose for our lives.

I believe the key to this story resides in verse 33: "there we saw the giants… and we were like grasshoppers in our own sight, and so we were in their sight." They saw themselves as grasshoppers in their own sight, which led them to believe their enemies would definitely see them as tiny bugs incapable of conquering the land. They doubted themselves first. This self-consciousness blurred their vision of what God guaranteed. Without a confident belief in who God proclaimed them to be, they were unable to understand the covenant they had with God. He promised them the land. He made a covenant with them, but they doubted. Who were they to doubt what God said about them? Who are we to doubt what God says about us? Their doubts kept them in the desert. Our doubts could keep us from the oasis of blessings God has on the horizon.

If we don't understand who we are in Christ, then we will forever view ourselves as grasshoppers. It's impossible to receive the blessings God's grace promises if we don't buy in to what He says about us. He has a purpose and He has a plan. He's promised both of these things to each of us. But, if we second guess what He's already declared over us and allow our vision to be blurred by self-doubt, then it's impossible to walk into the abundant life God has for us. In order to experience the fullness of life God has for us, we need to know who we are. We need to be secure in our identity as believers.

IF WE DON'T UNDERSTAND WHO WE ARE IN CHRIST, THEN WE WILL FOREVER VIEW OURSELVES AS GRASSHOPPERS.

PERFORMANCE-BASED IDENTITY

It's hard to realize who you are when you're using the wrong scaling system. We live in a world that judges people based on performance. We've talked about the performance-based mentality before, but to go even further, we live in a world where we are constantly defined by what we *do* rather than who we *are*. When you think of LeBron James, what's the first thing that comes to your mind? Basketball player. If I asked you who Denzel Washington was, you'd probably say actor. Our culture labels people based on their performance and accomplishments. Our society defines people based on what they do.

This doesn't just apply to famous people. What's one of the first questions we ask when we first meet someone? "What do you do?" The way people answer that question often provides evidence to support the claim we define ourselves by what we do. People almost always respond with something like, "I'm a businessman...I'm a mother...I'm a teacher...I'm a doctor." The formulaic answer is "I am *insert profession*." We define who we are by what we do. And who's to say what you do isn't a huge part of who you are? It most assuredly is. But, what happens when you define yourself as a businessman and then you lose your business? What happens to the athlete who shatters his knee? What happens to the mother once her kids grow up and move away? The problem with your identity being rooted in what you do rather than who you are is that things change. It's the very nature of most things to change. Change is inevitable, but losing your sense of self every time change strikes is avoidable by basing your identity in someone and something that never changes: The person God says you are.

Just as we are not defined by the careers we choose or the things we do, neither are we defined by our behavior. Rooting our identities in our failures and successes can be even more dangerous than finding our sense of self in the things we do. If someone struggles with alcohol addiction, they'll often say, "I'm an alcoholic." If someone lives on the streets, they call themselves homeless. If someone had a failed business, they say, "I'm a failure." If someone has repeated problems with the law, they're labeled a criminal. Those things may be a part of one's life, but they don't define the person. Being successful is fantastic and failing is not fun, but success and failure are both fleeting. God and His promises transcend time: they never change and they never fade. As long as you look at yourself through the lens of your achievements and/or shortcomings, then you'll never break free from an identity riddled with disappointment.

You were meant to define yourself according to who God says you are. In the kingdom of God, your identity is not rooted in your actions. It is not determined by your job or social status. To God, your identity is based solely on what happened to you the moment you received Christ. For example, I'm a Copron because I was born into the Copron family. I didn't have to pass any tests or behave a certain way to become a Copron. I was simply born into the Copron family. My identity as a Copron was determined by my birth, not by my behavior. The same goes within the Kingdom of God. That's why we say someone is "born again" when they accept and receive Christ (John 3:3). When you are born again, you're given a new identity. None of the things you've done and none of the things you'll do in the future determine who you are after salvation. Your identity is rooted in Him and Him alone once you're born again. "Therefore, if anyone is in Christ, he is a new creation; old things have passed away; behold, all things have become new" (2 Corinthians 5:17). Salvation is more than simply receiving forgiveness so you can go to heaven when you die. It's a total rebirth. At the moment of salvation, you become a new creation.

The problem is we still remember our old selves. And, even if we didn't, we'd definitely remember the time we failed last week or dwell on the times we will inevitably fail in the future.

Many believers see themselves as sinners because they still sin. They still do unrighteous things, so they think they're unrighteous. Despite reaching the point of salvation and accepting God's grace, they continue to base their identity on their behavior. Maybe this is you. Fortunately for us, in God's kingdom it's birth, not behavior, determines identity. That's why God doesn't call you a sinner. In fact, He calls you a saint (1 Corinthians 1:2). God doesn't call you unrighteous. He says you're the righteousness of God in Christ (2 Corinthians 5:21). Your behavior doesn't determine your identity. You are who God says you are.

YOUR BEHAVIOR DOESN'T DETERMINE YOUR IDENTITY. YOU ARE WHO GOD SAYS YOU ARE.

Israel didn't enter the Promised Land because they saw themselves as helpless grasshoppers next to the giants. If you view yourself as a grasshopper, then you'll live life from a grasshopper's perspective. The giants never stopped the Israelites from entering the Promised Land. They didn't have to stop them. The Israelites stopped themselves by doubting their own identity. It was how they viewed themselves that held them back. If they had seen themselves through God's promise, then they'd have had the courage to go forward and claim victory. Instead, they allowed themselves to be defeated by doubt.

Forty years later, Joshua and Caleb (the only two spies who brought back positive reports) were getting ready to enter the Promised Land for the second time. Joshua was now in charge of the people. Like Moses, he sent a couple spies to investigate the land. The spies stayed at the home of a woman named Rahab. While housing the spies, Rahab spoke to them, "I know that the Lord has given you the land, that the terror of you has fallen on us, and that all the inhabitants of the land are fainthearted because of you. For we have heard how the Lord dried up the water of the Red Sea for you when you came out of Egypt, and what you did to the two kings of the Amorites who were on the other side of the Jordan, Sihon and Og, whom you utterly destroyed. And as soon as we heard these things, our hearts melted; neither did there remain any more courage in anyone because of you, for the Lord your God, He is God in heaven above and on earth beneath" (Joshua 2:9-11).

The first time the Israelites arrived at the Promised Land the inhabitants quaked with fear. They were terrified of God's people. They heard tales of their victories and shivered with fright at the impending attack. But the attack never came. The enemy had more confidence in the Israelites than they had in themselves. It took forty more years of desert wandering and a new leader in Joshua before the Israelites realized who they were in God and claimed the Promised Land. I think this same sort of thing happens to believers far too often. Your enemy knows who you are. He knows the authority and power that is yours through Christ. But, if *you* don't know who you are, then that promised power won't do you any good. It's only when you know your identity in Christ you live by the power. Then and only then, will you walk with the boldness and confidence of God, ready to take your Promised Land.

We're free from the law and our behavior
no longer determines our identity.
Our identity is now based "in Christ."

CHAPTER ELEVEN

IN CHRIST

IN CHRIST

CHAPTER ELEVEN

Of all the games we play as children, there's one that stands above the rest. I'd be willing to wager every kid has either played it or will at some point. It takes little to no skill; it's easy, fun, and anyone can play. I'm talking, of course, about Hide and Seek. From playing peak-a-boo with a baby, to searching cabinets for a contorted kid, it seems we've all played the game at some point. It's an absolute classic. It was certainly a classic for me and the street kids of Las Vegas. But there came a time when we no longer felt as though the game was age-appropriate, so we did what kids who outgrow a game do—we gave the game a little rule update.

First, we had to expand the boundaries. No longer would we be bound by one backyard. Instead, we'd extend the area of the game to include the entire block. Second, we decided we'd wait to play until it was dark, our paths lit only by the moon and street lamps. Lastly, we renamed the game. This was a must. Hide and Seek was for little kids. What we were playing was not "Hide and Seek." It was *Ditch 'Em*. When the sun finally set, our entire crew (minus the seeker) would take off into the night, searching for the best hiding spot our block had to offer. Once the seeker finished counting, the hunt was on. Each person who found was added to the seeking party. So, as the seeker located hiders, the search party grew until only one person was left. The last man standing won the game.

Over time the intensity of the game grew. With each game of *Ditch 'Em*, the stakes got a little higher. One evening I ran to the edge of our block's boundaries. There, I found a long row of hedges to provide the perfect cover. Now, while most kids would be content climbing a bush, crawling under it, or simply getting behind the hedges, I wasn't going to risk being denied victory that night. I jumped directly into the bush, burrowing deep into the heart of the thicket. The search commenced as I tried to steady my breath. One by one my friends were found, and I was the only one still hiding. As I lay in a blanket of branches, I knew victory was mine, but I wouldn't relent until the game was punctuated with cries of surrender from my friends.

At one point, they found my bush. A couple of my compadres crept within mere inches of my face. One of them even spread some of my branches. I thought for sure I'd be found, but it was like I had stealth cloaking. Even as I lay motionless before them, they couldn't see me. They only saw the bush.

Just as I was fully covered by the limbs and leaves of that bush, so too are we clothed in the righteousness of Jesus Christ. Upon accepting Him, all of our failures, inadequacies, and shortcomings are hidden in Christ.

> *For you died, and your life is now hidden with Christ in God (Colossians 3:1-3).*

> *Or do you not know that as many of us as were baptized into Christ Jesus were baptized into His death? Therefore, we were buried with Him through baptism into death, that just as Christ was raised from the dead by the glory of the Father, even so we also should walk in newness of life" (Romans 6:3-4).*

When you're saved, you're more than just forgiven. You're baptized into Christ. That means when He died, you died. When He was buried, you were buried. When He was raised to life, you were raised with Him. Romans 5 describes how the entire world is either "in Adam" or "in Christ." So, when you come to faith through Jesus, you're no longer in Adam but in

Christ. The Bible talks a lot about this spiritual shift transpiring when one comes to Christ. At the moment of salvation, the sinner is plucked out of darkness and placed into the light (1 Peter 2:9). We were taken away from the powers of evil and placed into the Kingdom of Christ (Colossians 1:13). The Bible describes this spiritual shift as being "in Christ," or "in Him." Here are just a handful of times The Bible mentions it:

> *For in Him we live and move and have our being (Acts 17:28).*

> *For in Him dwells all the fullness of the Godhead bodily; and you are complete in Him"(Colossians 2:9-10).*

> *Blessed be the God and Father of our Lord Jesus Christ, who has blessed us with every spiritual blessing in the heavenly places in Christ (Ephesians 1:3).*

> *Even when we were dead in trespasses, made us alive together with Christ (by grace you have been saved), and raised us up together, and made us sit together in the heavenly places in Christ Jesus (Ephesians 2:5-6).*

The New Testament is filled with the phrase "in Christ."

These passages reinforce the idea that our identity isn't performance-based. It is now based "in Christ." "For all of you who were baptized into Christ have clothed yourselves with Christ" (Galatians 3:27). Upon salvation we're clothed in Christ. So, when God the Father looks at us, He sees Jesus. He doesn't see our flaws, imperfections, or sins. Grace allows us to be in Christ. Jesus provided the perfect lens through which God sees us.

Since you're in Christ, whatever is true of Him is now true of you. Is Christ fully accepted by God? Yep. Is Christ righteous? You bet. Is He without spot or blemish? Yes and yes. Is Christ loved? You already know it! Since Jesus Christ is all of those things, so are we upon accepting Him. You and I get Jesus Christ VIP treatment in the court of heaven thanks to His sacrifice.

God welcomes us not because of our performance or lack thereof but because Christ took care of everything on our behalf (Ephesians 1:6). As Christians, we're not made righteous by our own good deeds. We're righteous because we're in Christ (2 Corinthians 5:21). The New Testament says it over and over again. Ephesians 1:4 proclaims we're holy and without spot simply because Christ is blameless before God the Father. On the cross, Christ took on all of our sin, but when He rose from the dead, He was cleared of all sin. Therefore, we too are cleared thanks to Him (Ephesians 1:7). Forgiveness, righteousness, and acceptance don't come from some vending machine in heaven. They don't come because you try hard to live a holy life. All of these things are ours because we are "in Christ."

PERFECT HIGH PRIEST

While imperfect, there was a similar system in the Old Testament. Before Jesus gave us a gateway to God, there was the high priest. He was the guy who had the right to minister in the presence of God. On the Day of Atonement he entered the Holy of Holies, where God's presence resided, in order to represent the entire nation of Israel. The high priest was their representative before God. So, as the priest was before God, so too were the people. When Jesus came, He replaced the high priest, giving the people (us) a more direct way to come to God. "Therefore, in all things He had to be made like His brethren, that He might be a merciful and faithful High Priest in things pertaining to God, to make propitiation for the sins of the people" (Hebrews 2:17). Jesus became the sole High Priest, perfectly faithful in every aspect. His standing before God was and is perfect, which means our standing with God is also perfect. When God looks at you, He sees the perfect

WHEN GOD THE FATHER LOOKS AT US, HE SEES JESUS.

High Priest, Jesus Christ. We can't lose God's acceptance because Jesus stands blameless in our place, bridging the gap between God's welcoming arms and us.

Not only is Jesus the perfect High Priest, but He's also the perfect sacrifice. In the Old Testament, the Israelites had to bring sacrifices to the temple for atonement. The priest would examine their sacrifice for blemishes because in order for the sacrifice to be accepted by God, it had to be flawless (Leviticus 22:21). The priest didn't examine the person, only the animal they brought as an offering. If it passed the inspection, then the sacrifice was accepted. The Old Testament system of animal sacrifice was a preview of the perfect, everlasting sacrifice Jesus provides in the New Testament. The old system foreshadowed the final, flawless sacrifice Jesus would make on our behalf. So, just as the old animal had to be without flaw in order to be accepted, so too did Jesus have to walk this earth in flawless perfection in order to be accepted as the ultimate offering for mankind.

> For the law, having a shadow of the good things to come, and not the very image of the things, can never with these same sacrifices, which they offer continually year by year, make those who approach perfect. For then would they not have ceased to be offered? For the worshipers, once purified, would have had no more consciousness of sins. But in those sacrifices there is a reminder of sins every year. For it is not possible that the blood of bulls and goats could take away sins (Hebrews 10:1-4).

The blood of bulls and goats couldn't really take away sin.

It was only a sneak peek of what Christ would ultimately come and do for us. He was and is the only perfect offering for sin, which is why His sacrificial grace completely removes all sin. Jesus Christ is both our perfect High Priest and flawless sacrifice. That's why Hebrews 10:14 says, "for by one offering He has perfected forever those who are being sanctified." Through His death you've been forever changed. You've been made perfect in the eyes of God. You aren't perfect for a mere moment after you ask for forgiveness. You aren't perfect until you inevitably sin again. You're perfect forever through Him. There's nothing you can do to add or subtract from your standing with God. Now, that doesn't mean we'll have perfect behavior or a flawless track record. That's not what the Word says. It says we're perfect through our identity in Christ. Through Jesus we have been made totally and completely acceptable in God's eyes. Hebrews 5:6 says Jesus' priesthood is eternal. And, since His reign is without end and we are in Him, then we have been made blameless forever through Him.

POSITION VERSUS CONDITION

While Christ made us blameless in God's sight, we're still being made holy on a day-to-day basis. None of us live the perfect life only Christ was capable of living. So while our position is perfect, our condition is fluid, meaning it's constantly changing, depending on our actions. Thankfully, God meets with us based on the position Christ secured for us rather than the condition we create for ourselves. He deals with us on the basis of our being in Christ. This idea is presented throughout The Bible, but I love the way the NIV translates Hebrews 10:14: "For by one sacrifice He has made perfect forever those who are being made holy." So, while our position is forever perfect, our condition is steadily being made more holy. Jesus ensured our right standing with God through His sacrifice, but our condition is constantly in the process of becoming more like Jesus. Our position is consistent, but our condition is in flux. Sometimes we reflect our identity in Christ and other times we fall short of His plan for us. Regardless, our condition has no effect on our position. Thankfully for us, it's through the consistent position of right standing that God the Father interacts with us.

GOD MEETS WITH US BASED ON THE POSITION CHRIST SECURED FOR US RATHER THAN THE CONDITION WE CREATE FOR OURSELVES.

Forgiveness is a present tense reality that enables us to concentrate on walking with God. It frees us from the guilt of the past so we might be able to live fully in the present.

COMPLETE FORGIVENESS

COMPLETE FORGIVENESS

CHAPTER TWELVE

There are so many dimensions to God's grace, but of all the aspects of the grace-based faith we've discussed thus far, the idea of complete forgiveness tends to be the most controversial. If you've made it all the way to chapter twelve, then you're probably going to see this thing through to the end. You should know, though, the ideas unpacked in this chapter have not only brought the most freedom from guilt, shame, and condemnation, but they've also riled up the most people during my time as a minister. It's remarkably sad how many Christians live under the weight of perpetual guilt for sins they've committed in the past. Some people live their entire lives burdened by regret and shame caused by some sin they committed years ago. I once taught a message on grace and God's complete forgiveness, and at the end of the service, a man in his late fifties approached me. He told me how he'd been living under constant condemnation for things he'd done as a young man of about eighteen years. He'd once had a desire to go into ministry, but he felt like the sins of his past disqualified him from being used by God. With his eyes glossy with tears, he thanked me for the newfound freedom he'd discovered. Years later, that same man now pastors a church.

Have you ever felt like that man, like you're disqualified from the Kingdom of God because of your past? Or maybe you feel like God doesn't want to use you because of the mistakes you've made. I used to feel I couldn't be used by God because of the constant failures in my walk with Christ. If you've ever felt this sort of nagging guilt and condemnation, then you've yet to fully realize, understand, and accept the complete and total forgiveness freely given by Jesus Christ. In this chapter, I hope to highlight the incredible depth of God's complete forgiveness, so you may come to a more complete understanding of the freedom from guilt and condemnation that is yours through Jesus Christ.

> *But also for this very reason, giving all diligence, add to your faith virtue, to virtue knowledge, to knowledge self-control, to self-control perseverance, to perseverance godliness, to godliness brotherly kind-*

ness, and to brotherly kindness love. For if these things are yours and abound, you will be neither barren nor unfruitful in the knowledge of our Lord Jesus Christ. For he who lacks these things is short-sighted, even to blindness, and has forgotten that he was cleansed from his old sins (2 Peter 1:5-9).

In this passage Peter addresses our spiritual growth. Growing in faith, knowledge, love, and self-control are all qualities that should become more and more evident in our lives as we mature in our relationship with God. If we lack these characteristics, it's because we've forgotten that we've been cleansed from our old sins. If ever we find our love lacking, our self-control breaking down, or our faith faltering, it is because we've forgotten our forgiveness. Failure to recognize the sin issue between you and God has been dealt with will stunt your spiritual growth. It will hinder you from growing in God. Therefore, it's crucial for us to understand the total forgiveness we have through Jesus Christ.

In his book, *Classic Christianity*, Bob George says, "Forgiveness isn't just some doctrine that allows us to slip into heaven some day; God's forgiveness is a present tense reality that enables us to concentrate on walking with God today!" If we're still focusing on our past failures, mistakes, and sins, then we'll miss what God wants to do in our lives in the here and now. Focusing on a past that's already been taken care of is like trying to drive a car solely using the rear-view mirror. If you're trying to move forward in life, but you're still looking at what lies behind you, then you'll constantly crash into things.

How much of your prayer time is consumed by forgiveness pleas? If apologies comprise the bulk of your prayer time, then something is wrong. I'm not saying it isn't healthy to admit when we're wrong and own our mistakes. I'm just questioning the logic behind devoting the majority of our prayer time to asking for a forgiveness that Jesus already gave us.

I was mentoring a young man once who told me he didn't want to pray because every time he finished praying he felt depressed. I asked him what his prayer time consisted of. Unfortunately, his answer was far too common. His prayer time was basically him harping on his failures. I told him his feelings of post-prayer sorrow were rooted in the fact that he wasn't actually praying. All he was doing was talking to God about how terrible he was. I said, "Instead of whining to God about how worthless you are, just start praising God for the fact that no matter how much of a screw up you are He still loves you. Instead of focusing on all your failures, focus on His grace and goodness." Sure enough, the bouts of post-prayer depression subsided as soon as this young man stopped focusing on his faults and started proclaiming God's goodness. Forgiveness is a present tense reality enabling us to concentrate on walking with God. It frees us from

IF WE'RE STILL FOCUSING ON OUR PAST FAILURES, MISTAKES, AND SINS, THEN WE'LL MISS WHAT GOD WANTS TO DO IN OUR LIVES IN THE HERE AND NOW.

the guilt of the past so we might be able to live fully in the present. Until you realize the sin issue between you and God has already been handled, you'll never be able to move forward and grow in God.

UNDERSTANDING FORGIVENESS

So, what exactly does complete forgiveness mean, and how is it different from the common understanding of forgiveness? The most common (mis)understanding of forgiveness within the Christian faith goes something like this: You come to Christ, you're saved by His grace, and all of your past sins are washed away. But the sins you have yet to commit haven't been dealt with yet, so now, every time you sin you need to ask God for forgiveness. Whenever you ask God for forgiveness, He wipes your slate clean again, but then your sins start adding up until the next time you ask to be forgiven. That's how most Christians understand forgiveness.

Some denominations take things a step further, arguing that if you die with any unconfessed sins in your life, you immediately go to hell. Regardless of how much you love the Lord, how long you've lived honestly, or how much you love others, one single sin can doom you to hell if it goes unconfessed. While this belief is a bit more extreme than most, 99% of Christians misunderstand forgiveness to a certain degree.

While it may sound too good to be true, the New Testament proclaims when we come to faith God forgives our past, present, and future sins. That's the gospel. That's the good news. That's grace. It's not like there's a forgiveness bank in Heaven from which we must constantly withdraw in order to get right with God. Take a look at what Ephesians has to say about forgiveness: "In Him we have redemption through His blood, the forgiveness of sins, according to the riches of His grace" (Ephesians 1:7). If we are in Christ, then we have forgiveness. Forgiveness is a present tense reality. It's not something we have certain days and don't have other days. If you are in Christ, then you live in a continual state of forgiveness.

IF YOU ARE IN CHRIST, THEN YOU LIVE IN A CONTINUAL STATE OF FORGIVENESS.

1 John takes things a step further in explaining God's forgiveness: "but if we walk in the light as He is in the light, we have fellowship with one another, and the blood of Jesus Christ His Son cleanses us from all sin" (1 John 1:7). Once again we see the word "cleanses" in the present tense, indicating a continuous action. Therefore, the moment you come to Christ the blood of Jesus cleanses you from all sin, and it continues to cleanse you.

I heard a story about a boy who lived in a third world country. One day, he found this big, beautiful diamond. He was going to take it home, but he knew if anyone else saw it they would have stolen it. So he went and buried it in the ground. Whenever he wanted to see it he would dig it up, wash it off, and behold the beauty of his gem. He did this over and over everyday. One day, when he was washing the diamond near a local waterfall, he had an idea. Instead of burying the diamond in the ground and washing it off every time he wanted to see it, he could hide it under the waterfall so it would stay continually clean. He found a little spot under the waterfall and hid the rock where the water constantly cascaded over the diamond, leaving it spotless.

Many Christians take the same approach to forgiveness that the boy first took with his diamond. They view themselves as something dirty that needs to be cleaned over and over again. But the forgiveness the Bible tells us about is just like the constant cleansing of the waterfall. We are the boy's diamond and Jesus has offered us a spot under His waterfall, so that we might be continually cleansed every moment of everyday. Once you put your faith in Jesus, you are placed under the waterfall of God's forgiveness and mercy where you are forever cleansed.

"When you were dead in your sins and in the uncircumcision of your flesh, God made you alive with Christ. He forgave us all our sins" (Colossians 2:13). How many of our sins does Colossians say are forgiven? *All* of them. In the original Greek language the word *all* means "all." That's it. There's nothing lost in translation. There's no loophole or different definition. The Bible says *all* of our sins are forgiven, past, present, and future. God isn't keeping a record of your sins or adding them up until you ask for forgiveness. 1 Corinthians 13 proclaims, "love keeps no record of wrongs." God is love, therefore He keeps no record of your wrongdoing. When God looks at you, He sees you as completely forgiven. You stand before Him as if you never sinned.

CONFESSION AND FORGIVENESS

If you embrace the truth that you've been completely forgiven of all your past, present, and future sins, you then realize your forgiveness isn't dependent upon your confession. I was taught, like most Christians, if you didn't confess your sins, God couldn't or wouldn't forgive you. This teaching would mean forgiveness is dependent upon our confession, not His grace. The whole system of receiving forgiveness solely through confession is riddled with problems. What happens if you forget about a sin and it goes forever unconfessed? Are you doomed for eternity because you forgot you sinned that one time? Of course not. Our forgiveness is not reliant upon our confession, but upon God's grace.

Remember too, sins aren't just the bad things you do, they're also the good things you fail to do. "Therefore, to him who knows to do good and does not do it, to him it is sin" (James 4:17). Now, by the forgiveness through confession logic, you have to confess sins of omission and commission. Trying to keep track of all your sins to ensure you stay forgiven is enough to give anyone, good or bad, a nervous breakdown. This sort of lifestyle forces you to focus on your failures rather than God's grace. The goal of the finished work of Jesus is to bring you to a place where you're not even conscious of sin anymore (Hebrews 10:1-3).

To clarify, I'm not saying I don't believe in confession. I believe confession is a healthy spiritual practice creating openness and transparency with God. I just don't believe I have to confess my sins in order to be forgiven because I am already forgiven. If your child does something wrong, do you wait until they apologize to forgive them? Sure, it might upset you a bit they were disobedient in the first place, but you don't hold out on forgiving a child because he or she fails to ask for forgiveness. As a loving parent, you forgive regardless of confession. Now, does a confession help to nurture and grow your relationship through honesty and transparency? Sure! But the relationship isn't based solely on the confession, and neither is forgiveness.

Consider again the account of the prodigal son in Luke 15. When the younger, wayward brother decided to return home to see if his father would take him back as a hired servant, he prepared this apology speech: "Father, I am no more worthy to be called your son. Make me like one of your hired servants." The passage goes on to say, "but as the younger son was still a long way off, the father saw him and ran after him." As soon as the younger son saw his father, he went into his rehearsed speech: "Father, I am no more worthy to be called your son." But the father didn't even let him finish the speech before grabbing him in a huge hug. The father didn't wait for his son to confess or apologize. He didn't even seem interested in the well-worded speech. He'd already forgiven his son long before the son decided to return home.

Confession is intended to be a simple act of open honesty with God about your shortcomings, sins, flaws, and failures. The word *confession* means "to say the same thing as."[8] Confession is calling something as it is. When you know you did wrong, you call it as it is. You own up to it and admit your failure. When I sin I say, "God, I know this behavior is not in line with who You've called me to be or how You want me to live, but I thank You for paying for this sin on the cross," and then I go back to living my life. I'm not minimizing my sin; I'm glorifying God by thanking Him for His grace. It's like when a basketball player commits a foul. The referee blows the whistle to alert everyone someone has broken a rule, and then you usually see a player raise his hand, indicating he was the culprit who committed the foul. The referee already knew it, the fans already knew it, but the player is just making things quicker and easier by acknowledging it. He owns up to the foul and the game carries on. Confession is something I do because I'm forgiven, not something I do in order to be forgiven.

> **CONFESSION IS INTENDED TO BE A SIMPLE ACT OF OPEN HONESTY WITH GOD ABOUT YOUR SHORTCOMINGS, SINS, FLAWS, AND FAILURES.**

Forgiveness isn't dependent upon our confessions, but upon the riches of His grace (Ephesians 1:7). Think about it. Doesn't God expect us to forgive others even if they never ask for our forgiveness or admit they wronged us? He expects us to forgive regardless of confession because that's how He forgives. Do we really believe God expects us to operate in greater mercy and grace than He does? Certainly not. God isn't going to ask us to do something He Himself isn't willing to do. You are not more forgiving or compassionate than God is. I assure you.

The waterfall of grace given to us through God's complete forgiveness often scares or enrages people. I don't want you to get the wrong idea. I'm not trying to make light of sin. Sin is serious. In fact, sin is so serious that every single one had to be paid for by Jesus on the cross. The word says, "the Lord has laid on him the iniquity of us all" (Isaiah 53:6). God didn't cut any corners or sweep any sin under the rug. Every single sin was laid upon Jesus so we could be fully and completely forgiven. That's how serious sin is.

has light with darkness" (2 Corinthians 6:14)? Maybe confession and cleansing are only mentioned together once because this verse was intended for unbelievers, not as a commandment for believers to continually confess in order to be made right with God. Paul calls the believer righteous and the unbeliever lawless in this passage. The church of Corinth was involved in gross immorality. These were people living in sin, yet they were still believers. Paul refers to them as righteous because that's how God sees all believers.

1 John goes on to mention what the believer should do if they happen to stumble and sin. Chapter two says, "my little children, these things I write to you, so that you may not sin. And if anyone sins, we have an advocate with the Father, Jesus Christ The Righteous. And He Himself is the propitiation for our sins, and not for ours only but also for the whole world" (1 John 2:1-2). It doesn't say, "if anyone sins make sure you confess so you'll be forgiven." Paul explains Jesus Christ is our advocate with the Father, and He is the propitiation for our sins. *Propitiation* means, "the satisfying of wrath."[9] Therefore, when Christ died on the cross, He satisfied the wrath of God. What are we supposed to do when we sin? We're simply supposed to remember Jesus Christ is our advocate with the Father and He's already paid for our sin through His sacrifice on the cross.

I've heard other interpretations of this verse argue that we can only receive forgiveness when "we walk in the light as He is in the light." While 1 John 1:7 does say "if we walk in the light as He is in the light, we have fellowship with one another, and the blood of Jesus Christ His Son cleanses us from all sin," the passage isn't demanding we live up to a certain standard of holiness in order to attain right-standing. If that were what this verse was saying, then you'd have to walk as holy as God does in order to be cleansed. And, if that were indeed

JESUS CHRIST IS OUR ADVOCATE WITH THE FATHER AND HE'S ALREADY PAID FOR OUR SIN THROUGH HIS SACRIFICE ON THE CROSS.

the case, if you really managed to live as holy as Christ did, then you wouldn't need any cleansing or forgiveness anyway, right?

2 Peter continues to examine God's continual, eternal grace: "but you are a chosen generation, a royal priesthood, a holy nation, His own special people, that you may proclaim the praises of Him who called you out of darkness into His marvelous light" (2 Peter 2:9). This verse states, as a Christian who has accepted Christ, you've already been called out of darkness and into His light, and "what fellowship has light with darkness" (2 Corinthians 6:14)? If you're a believer, then you are light. "For you were once darkness, but now you are light in the Lord. Walk as children of light" (Ephesians 5:8). We were once in darkness, but, when we chose to believe the gospel and confess our need for a savior, we came out of darkness and into the light, where the blood of Jesus Christ continuously cleanses us from all sin. So, stop striving to be forgiven through your efforts and confessions, and just rest in the waterfall of forgiveness that continually washes over you.

Another arguable objection to God's complete forgiveness I want to address occurs in Matthew 6. People tend to mention that Jesus Himself said, "if you forgive men their trespasses, your heavenly Father will also forgive you. But, if you do not forgive men their trespasses, neither will your Father forgive your trespasses" (Matthew 6:14-15). Much of Jesus' ministry was to those under the law. Jesus often used his sermons to show people who thought they had met the requirements of the law just how short they'd fallen. In doing this, Jesus highlighted Himself as the way, the truth, and the light.

You see, Jesus was teaching on the Old Covenant truth as He prepared the way for the New Covenant. The Old Covenant states: forgive and you'll be forgiven. The motivation for forgiving others under the New Covenant, however, is completely different. "And be kind to one another, tenderhearted, forgiving one another, even as God in Christ forgave you" (Ephesians 4:32). The Bible beckons us to bear "with one another, forgiving one another, if anyone has a complaint against another; even as Christ forgave you, so you also must do" (Colossians 3:13). Over and over again we're told to forgive as we have been forgiven. In Christ, we've been forgiven for every sin. In the same way, God wants us to unconditionally forgive others. So, while the Old Covenant stated we should forgive in order to be forgiven, in the New Covenant, we're called to forgive because we have already been forgiven. The motivation is completely different. We don't forgive out of fear; we forgive because we have received an incredible, complete forgiveness ourselves, a forgiveness so grand we should extend that same grace to others!

Altering the motivation for forgiving others doesn't minimize the act of forgiveness at all. Forgiving others is extremely important. Very few things are more harmful to your health than holding grudges and harboring resentment. Unforgiveness can affect your physical, emotional, and spiritual well-being. The only things unforgiveness brings into your life are bondage and torment. It's imperative to forgive those who have hurt or offended you, but it's also helpful to understand we should be forgiving others from a place of grace rather than fear. While forgiveness under the Old Covenant may have been rooted in a fear of being punished, forgiveness in the New Covenant comes as a result of passing on the love and mercy God first showed us through His grace.

THE ONLY THINGS UNFORGIVENESS BRINGS INTO YOUR LIFE ARE BONDAGE AND TORMENT.

FUTURE SINS?

It's hard enough for people to understand Jesus has set them free from their past and current sins, but it's even harder to buy into the fact, through Christ, we've been forgiven for our future failures. How could God forgive us for the sins we've yet to commit? The answer is simple—when Jesus died on the cross, all of your sins were future sins! You weren't even born yet, but He was already taking on all of humanity's past, present, and future sin. He paid the price in full for every single sin through His sacrifice on the cross. Therefore, you have complete forgiveness from all sin— past, present and future.

You might be wondering just what happens when we sin if we're already forgiven. In Romans 4, Paul quotes Psalm chapter thirty-two, which just so happens to be one of the most incredible verses on forgiveness. "Blessed are those whose lawless deeds are forgiven, and whose sins are covered; blessed is the man to whom the Lord shall not impute sin" (Romans 4:7-8). Paul quotes the Psalm David originally wrote about the day when all of man's sin would be paid for in full. David saw there would soon be a permanent payment for all past, present, and future sin. His song foreshadows the coming of the New Covenant reality Paul imparted to the Romans, which we still live under today.

Let's further investigate Romans 4:7-8. The verse says, "blessed is the man to whom the Lord shall not impute sin." The word *blessed* here means "happy,"[10] and the word *impute* means "to charge or credit."[11] When you go shopping and use your credit card, the items you purchased are charged to your card. That money is imputed to your account, and there's a debt that must be paid. But, unlike American Express, this verse says when you slip up and go on a sin shopping spree, the Lord doesn't charge your account. Even when we do wrong, those sins aren't imputed unto us. The word *not* in this verse means "never, certainly not, not at all, by no means."[12] So really, this verse could translate as something like this: "Happy is the man to whom the Lord will never, by any means, credit for sin." Now that's reason for excitement! Even when we sin up a storm, God doesn't charge that sin to our account because all our sins were imputed to Jesus on the cross. What good news!

IT IS FINISHED

> *And when you were dead in your transgressions and the uncircumcision of your flesh, He made you alive together with Him, having forgiven us all our transgressions, having canceled out the certificate of debt consisting of decrees against us, and which was hostile to us; and He has taken it out of the way, having nailed it to the cross (Colossians 2:13-14 NASB).*

A certificate of debt was a contractual agreement between a debtor and a creditor. The word *teleo* means, "paid in full, fulfilled, or finished."[13] During Jesus' time on earth, this word was written on business documents and receipts to show a bill had been paid in full. When a debtor paid his debt, the lender took the certificate of debt and stamped it with the word *teleo*. They'd do something similar for criminals who'd served their time in prison. The charges against the person were nailed to the door of the person's prison cell, and when they'd served their time, their rap sheet was taken down and stamped with the word *teleo* to show the person's debt to society had been fulfilled. As long as that person had that certificate, they couldn't again be punished for that crime because their dues were paid.

Colossians says the certificate of debt containing all of our sins was nailed to the cross where Jesus took all of the punishment and penalty for our sin. When Jesus paid our debt in full, He cried out from the cross, "it is finished" (John 19:30). Do you know what the Greek word is for "finished"? *Teleo*: paid in full. He used His final breath to declare our debt paid. You have been cleared of all charges. The next time you feel guilt, shame, or condemnation from a sin you've committed, just remember: "It is finished." Teleo. Your sin has been paid in full.

RIGHTEOUSNESS MEANS YOU ARE
WELCOMED INTO THE PRESENCE OF GOD
AS IF YOU WERE JESUS.

THE GIFT OF RIGHTEOUSNESS

THE GIFT OF RIGHTEOUSNESS

CHAPTER FOURTEEN

I grew up in a golden age. A time before smart phones, Facebook friends, and freemium games. It was a world where kids could play outside, and actually wanted to… until the modern wonder of my world was invented. Throughout the course of human history incredible inventions have emerged and altered the universe, from the wheel to the light bulb, from penicillin to the printing press, from the compass to the Nintendo. That's right. I grew up during the reign of the original Nintendo. I played my childhood days away with Mario, Double Dragon, and Tecmo Bowl (a game where the coders literally made a player unbeatable). If ever you find yourself in a hazy den competing for your life in a Tecmo Bowl tournament, choose the Raiders and run with Bo Jackson. Unstoppable.

But above all of these classic games reigns the king of cartridges, the game I'd spend countless hours cleaning with my breath just to get a few more minutes of Nintendo nirvana. The game was "Mike Tyson's Punch Out." Just in case you've lived an existence deprived of this great game, here's the premise: You're a young, up-and-coming boxer who has to fight fictional characters as you rise through the ranks of the boxing world in order to get a chance at taking on Tyson. As I bobbed and weaved my way toward a digital boxing brawl with Iron Mike, I came across a fighter called King Hippo. This guy was the bane of my young existence. He's one of the toughest characters on the game. Whereas previous bouts all dealt with blasting buttons as fast as possible, the fight with King Hippo was more about strategy. You can only punch this guy when his mouth is open. He blocks any combinations thrown while his mouth is closed. This fat fighter drove me mad until the destined day I discovered his weakness. King Hippo had an Achilles heel of sorts. If I could just bide my time and strike him when his mouth was open, then eventually I'd knock him down, and, since King Hippo was a big boy, he couldn't get up once you knocked him down. Fight over.

You're probably wondering why I'm detailing my bouts with King Hippo and "Mike Tyson's Punch Out." First, it's just a fantastic game. But more importantly, I think King Hippo is a great metaphor for our spiritual lives. I've met a lot of King Hippo Christians who have a great defense against the enemy's strategies, but when they get knocked down, and we all get knocked down eventually, they don't know how to get up. They stay on the mat while the accuser counts to ten, eliminating them from the competition. These King Hippo Christians can't get up because they don't know the gift of righteousness they received when they gave their lives to Jesus. "For a righteous man falls seven times, and rises again" (Proverbs 24:16 NASB). The righteous man can fall seven times and still get up. When you know you're the righteousness of God in Christ, you'll keep getting back up, regardless of how many times you fall. Understanding our identity as the righteousness of God is essential to conquering guilt, shame, and condemnation.

Every time I teach on righteousness I like to ask the listeners a few questions. First, I ask, by a show of hands, how many are as righteous as me? Most of the time the people know me, so most of the hands shoot toward the sky. Next, I ask how many are as righteous as Paul the Apostle? Not as many hands go up in response to this question. Finally, I ask how many believe they're as righteous as Jesus Christ? No hands rise from the listeners' laps. Although most believers walk around unaware, we're as righteous as Jesus Christ. Through grace, we've been made as righteous as Jesus.

I used to cringe at the thought of a message on righteousness. Growing up, all these sermons made me feel guilty. I've always had a sensitive conscience so it's never taken much for me to glide down guilt street, but those messages on righteousness were especially good at making me feel like I was worthless. Without fail, these guilt trips were followed by an altar call: A plea to come down and confess in order to live a righteous life. The pastors called for repentance from the unrighteous and a promise to God that we'd be better.

How many of you have ever been in a church service where you promised God you'd live a life more dedicated to him? How many times have you assured him you were done with a certain sin? If you're anything like me, then you've done this quite a few times… and then by Wednesday you'd already stumbled and sinned again. After the guilt sets in, you repent, you pray, you promise to do better, and the vicious cycle repeats itself again and again. Variations of this sinful cycle continue to plague the Christian life, but I've got some good news. Things don't have to be this way. You don't have to feel like you failed yourself, and, even worse, feel like you failed God.

The devil has a heyday with Christians shackled by misconceptions of righteousness. In the book of Revelation, the devil is called the "accuser of the brethren" (Revelation 12:10). His main job is to accuse believers of their sins, and, when we don't understand our righteousness, we fall for his accusations and succumb

WHEN WE DON'T UNDERSTAND OUR RIGHTEOUSNESS, WE FALL FOR HIS ACCUSATIONS AND SUCCUMB TO CONDEMNATION.

to condemnation. Weighed down by our inadequacies and an inability to see Christ took care of these things long ago, we tend to try to better ourselves through our own futile devices. No matter how much we pray, rededicate our lives, read The Bible, or go to church, there will always be a lingering sense of guilt until we understand the righteousness we have in Jesus.

RIGHTEOUSNESS AND SELF-RIGHTEOUSNESS

The word righteousness means "right standing." If you're righteous, then you're in right standing with God. Some people think righteousness is something achieved through good behavior and an adherence to a set of rules. They believe if you do all the right things and don't do the bad, then you're righteous. The Scripture has a term for people who believe themselves to be righteous through their own works: Self-righteous or works-righteous. God has some very strong feelings about self-righteousness. In Isaiah 64 the Lord says, "all our righteousness are as filthy rags" (Isaiah 64:6). Everything we do in an attempt to earn right standing with God through our own works is as disgusting as "filthy rags." Now, "filthy rags" sounds bad enough, but the original Hebrew takes things a bit further. In Hebrew, the phrase "filthy rags"[14] refers to dirty menstrual cloths. With that image in mind, you can see The Lord does not appreciate the hubris that comes with the self-righteous, works-based mentality.

When The Bible condemns self-righteousness, it's denouncing the things we try to do on our own in order to gain right standing with God. While several scriptures are critical of self-righteousness, The Bible glorifies the gift of righteousness, otherwise known as faith-righteousness. Faith-righteousness is the opposite of self-righteousness. Take a look at a couple of these passages in which The Bible talks about the gift of righteousness through faith:

> *"For if by the one man's offense, death reigned through the one, much more those who receive abundance of grace and of the gift of righteousness will reign in life through the One, Jesus Christ" (Romans 5:17).*

> *"For He made Him who knew no sin to be sin for us, that we might become the righteousness of God in Him" (2 Corinthians 5:21).*

The gift of righteousness comes through faith in Christ. When Jesus died on the cross, He became sin for us. He embodied the very thing separating us from God in order to bring us into a right relationship with Him. He took upon Himself our sin so He could give us His righteousness. We now stand before God without any sense of guilt, shame, or condemnation. If Jesus Christ gave us His perfect standing with God, then we're welcomed into the presence of God as if we were

Jesus himself. Nothing we did brought us into a right relationship with God. Nothing we do in the future can make us more righteous. We can't earn a better standing with God than the one Jesus freely gave to us. Our righteousness has nothing to do with us in the first place, so there's nothing we can to do to mess it up.

There's a sort of real-life parable I believe symbolizes what God did for us through His Son. If a baby lamb's mother dies, then often times that baby lamb will try to latch onto another nearby mother sheep. However, the mother sheep needs only to sniff the baby lamb to realize the lamb isn't one of her own. She'll smell the outsider and push it away from her own, leaving it to die without milk or a mother's care. While shepherds soon discovered mother sheep aren't much into adoption, they also found if the baby lamb were to smell like the mother's other babies, then she'd accept the outsider. So, if one of her own happens to die, then often times shepherds will take the coat of the dead lamb and put it on the orphan lamb. The mother sheep smells what she believes to be her own and accepts the orphan.

That is a perfect picture of what God did for us. What did John the Baptist say when he saw Jesus? "John saw Jesus coming toward him and said, 'the lamb of God, which takes away the sin of the world'" (John 1:29). God sent his lamb into the world to die on our behalf, that we might be clothed in His righteous coat so our God, who is absolutely holy, could look on us and call us righteous and accepted like His Son. Thanks to Jesus' sacrifice we are no longer the orphaned lambs but completely accepted and clean in God's eyes. Doesn't that make you feel good? You've been made righteous by the grace of God apart from your works!

Through Adam's disobedience, we were made sinners, but in the same way, everyone who accepts Christ is made righteous.

CHAPTER FIFTEEN

NO LONGER A SINNER

NO LONGER A SINNER

CHAPTER FIFTEEN

Over the years, I've invited a lot of people to church. It's pretty incredible how often my invitation is met with people declaring their level of sinfulness. "Now, preacher, if I walked in your church, the whole roof would cave in," some will say. Others make comments about lightning striking them down or spontaneous combustion occurring. People don't seem to have any qualms about announcing the fact they're sinners. It seems to be an easy pill for people to swallow. People have a much more difficult time accepting their righteousness in Christ.

So many people fail to realize they've been made righteous through Christ, regardless of their actions. People walk around believing they're sinners saved by grace, but the truth of the matter is, while we *were once* sinners, Jesus saves by grace and makes us sinners *no more*. Sure, we still sin. We're human. Humans sin. Jesus does not sin. And, thanks to His sacrifice, to God we are as righteous as Jesus.

The message of our righteousness through Christ tends to get a rise out of people. I remember coming to the realization that God didn't see me as a sinner but as totally righteous, and being so hyped. I immediately took to the Scripture and drafted a message about His grace. When I delivered this message at a Bible study, I was met with some pretty serious backlash. I watched one man's face contort with contempt until his anger came to a crescendo. He blurted out, "Do you still sin?" I tried to level with him, replying, "Yes, of course." He smirked, believing I'd fallen into some sort of scriptural snare. "Well, if you still sin, then that makes you a sinner." The man sat back, pleased with his logic. Everyone in the room looked at me like, "This guy has a point." As calmly as I could, I asked the man how many sins it takes to be a sinner. He replied, "One," with confidence peaking. "Hm," I pondered aloud, "It's actually zero." I answered his quizzical look with a passage from Romans 5:

> For as by one man's disobedience many were made sinners, so also by one man's obedience many will be made righteous (Romans 5:19).

Because Adam sinned, we were all born sinners without ever committing a sin. We tend to believe the reverse: "Because you sin, you're a sinner." But really, we were born sinners. Sinners by birth. That's why we sin. If you've ever spent time around little children, you know this to be true! Through Adam's disobedience we were made sinners, but, in the same way, everyone who accepts Christ is made righteous. If you didn't have to do a righteous deed to become righteous, then you're not a sinner just because you sin. It's not about what you do. It's about what God has done for you.

Even though we've been made righteous, we still sin. Just because we might stumble in an area of sin doesn't mean we are still sinners. When you give your life to Christ, He doesn't take away your ability to sin. Instead, He just takes away your ability to fully enjoy your sin the way you once did.

I have spent years working with teenagers. I've noticed it doesn't matter how many times a student has responded to a call to accept Jesus as their Savior; if they're presented with the opportunity, they will often raise their hands or come forward again. It doesn't matter whether I specifically state that this particular opportunity is for those who've never accepted Christ. Some students, who I know to be saved, will still respond. Every time I talk to them about this they say things like, "Well, I don't really feel saved because I still commit some of the same sins I did before accepting Christ." Whenever someone says this, I always ask how they felt after committing those sins. They usually express feelings of guilt or shame. That's the key. If you feel terrible after you sin, then that seems like hard evidence to support your salvation. Most people don't feel too bad about sinning before they're saved. While we may still sin, the proof of our salvation and righteousness lies in our inability to enjoy the sins we once felt fine committing.

Hear me out—I still sin. All Christians still sin. But it's important for us to understand and address the terrible feelings that accompany those actions after salvation. Upon accepting God's gift of grace and entering into a state of righteousness through Christ, we're no longer sinners, regardless of our sin. That's why we feel crummy after sinning—because we're no longer sinners. It's not natural anymore. The most miserable people in the world are Christians who are living in sin because it goes against their new nature.

WHILE WE MAY STILL SIN, THE PROOF OF OUR SALVATION AND RIGHTEOUSNESS LIES IN OUR INABILITY TO ENJOY THE SINS WE ONCE FELT FINE COMMITTING.

THE HOLY SPIRIT

Through our journey into understanding Graceology, we've discussed the role of God the Father and God the Son, but now let us dig into the role of God the Holy Spirit. A lot of people believe the Holy Spirit's role is to provide us with conviction when we sin. Many Christians view the Holy Spirit as a sort of divine tattle-tell, constantly lurking in the shadows, always waiting and watching for us to mess up. But I'm here to tell you there isn't a verse in the Bible to support this theory. The Bible doesn't say anything about the Holy Spirit working in the conviction office of Holy Trinity, Inc. The Holy Spirit isn't here to point out your mistakes. Again, you can pour through the Scriptures, but there's nothing there that says it's the Holy Spirit's job to point out our flaws and heap guilt upon our consciences.

Now, I'm sure some of you Wizards of the Word are racking your brains for scriptures like the one saying, "the Holy Spirit convicts the world of sin." Well, let's actually take a look at that passage of Scripture:

> Nevertheless, I tell you the truth. It is to your advantage that I go away; for if I do not go away, the Helper will not come to you; but if I depart, I will send Him to you. And when He has come, He will convict the world of sin, and of righteousness, and of judgment: of sin, because they do not believe in Me; of righteousness, because I go to My Father and you see Me no more; of judgment, because the ruler of this world is judged (John 16:7-11).

Before we can fully unpack this verse and do it justice, we must understand what the word *convict* means in the context of this passage. When most people think of the word *conviction* in regards to religion, they think about that bad feeling they get in their gut whenever they sin or do something wrong. However, Strong's Concordance defines *convict* as a verb meaning "to convince."[15] Now, let's substitute the word *convince* for *convict* in John 16. After doing this, we see the Holy Spirit is here to convince people of sin, righteousness, and judgment. Still, you may be saying to yourself the verse plainly states the Holy Spirit is here to convince us of our sins. But when you read Verse 9 it says the Holy Spirit "will convince the world of sin… because they do not believe in me." The only people the Holy Spirit convicts or convinces of sin are unbelievers. The Holy Spirit comes alongside those who don't believe and convicts them of their unbelief so they can come to faith in Christ. He is here to help highlight the things are keeping unbelievers from receiving God's grace, not to make them feel bad for being sinful.

So, if the Holy Spirit is here to help unbelievers come to believe, then what about those of us who already believe? The role of the Holy Spirit in the life of the believer is to convince them of their righteousness in Christ. "Of righteousness, because I go to my Father and you see me no more." Again, our logic is backwards. For too long Christians have assumed the Holy Spirit is here to highlight our wicked ways. The truth is God gave us the Holy Spirit to help convince us we are righteous through Christ, regardless of our sins. Jesus took care of our sins, and now the Holy Spirit wants to highlight

THE ROLE OF THE HOLY SPIRIT IN THE LIFE OF THE BELIEVER IS TO CONVINCE THEM OF THEIR RIGHTEOUSNESS IN CHRIST.

our righteousness.

Remember, Satan is the accuser of the brethren. He's made it his mission to point out our sins in order to instill guilt, shame, and condemnation. We've mixed up the Holy Spirit's motives with those of Satan, allowing ourselves to be fooled by the enemy. It's not the Holy Spirit harping on our sins. It's that age-old foe making accusations and reminding us of sins for which we've already been forgiven. God says, "I will remember your sins no more" (Hebrews 8:12). Why then would He send the Holy Spirit to bring up sins He forgave and forgot? Father, Son, and Holy Spirit work together in perfect unity. Therefore, it makes no sense for God to wipe away all sin only to employ the Holy Spirit as a constant reminder of the very sins He handled on our behalf. That's not the work of the Holy Spirit. That's the work of the accuser, and, until we recognize it as the work of the enemy, we'll accept those accusations and remain in bondage.

I don't know about you, but I don't need anyone to convince me of my mistakes whenever I mess up. I get it. I don't need the Holy Spirit to rub my failures in my face. However, I do need the Holy Spirit to silence the attack of the enemy, to convince me I'm forgiven through Jesus Christ, and to remind me I'm still righteous thanks to His sacrifice. That's what the Holy Spirit is here to do in our lives. When we sin, the Holy Spirit comes along to remind us that, regardless of our sins, we are no longer sinners. The Holy Spirit is here to silence Satan and remind us of our righteousness in Christ.

The Bible describes the Holy Spirit as a comforter. That being said, no one finds comfort in having his or her mistakes pointed out. I think our misconceptions surrounding the Holy Spirit rest in a root of fear. Christians have painted a picture of the Holy Spirit as some sort of divine faultfinder, rather than a comforting encourager. The Holy Spirit is here to help, comfort, and console. Whenever we lose sight of who we are in Christ, the Holy Spirit comes along to convince us of our true identity. The Spirit serves as a reminder that our mistakes don't make us a mistake. Just because we fail doesn't mean we're failures. Our behavior doesn't determine our standing with God because we're freely forgiven and clothed in His righteousness.

AS A MAN THINKS IN HIS HEART

God provided us with the Holy Spirit so we might learn to live more like Jesus. As soon as we start seeing ourselves as righteous, we will begin to demonstrate righteous behavior. The Holy Sprit helps us realize our full potential. Contrary to popular belief, telling someone they're righteous, regardless of their sin, doesn't instigate or encourage a lifestyle of sin. The truth of the matter is once we begin to see ourselves as God does (righteous and forgiven), we'll begin to live more holy lives.

It's very difficult to be something you're not. If you believe yourself to be a sinner, striving to become more holy, then you'll continually fall short. In fact, your behavior will never line up with your new Christ-like identity until you start seeing yourself the way God sees you. "For, as he thinks in his heart, so is he" (Proverbs 23:7 KJV). Our behavior will always reflect the way we see ourselves, so the more we renew our minds to the reality that we are righteous in Christ, the more our lives will reflect that reality.

The key to righteous living is accepting and believing you are righteous in Christ. Condemning people for their sins doesn't produce holiness; it only creates a greater awareness of the faults and failures we all have in our lives. Knowing you've become the righteousness of God is the key to living a righteous life. Even when you struggle with sin and addiction, you're still righteous. There's nothing you did to deserve your righteous standing before God, so there's nothing you can do to lose it. You can keep on sinning and you'll never lose your righteousness. But once you're convinced of your righteousness, you won't want to keep sinning because it's no longer in line with the person you've become. Knowing we are the righteousness of God gives us the necessary empowerment to live out our true identity. When we're aware of Christ as our righteousness, we can stand before God without any sense of guilt, shame

CONDEMNING PEOPLE FOR THEIR SINS DOESN'T PRODUCE HOLINESS; IT ONLY CREATES A GREATER AWARENESS OF THE FAULTS AND FAILURES WE ALL HAVE IN OUR LIVES.

or condemnation, even on our worst days. Know that you are righteous not because of anything you've done but because of what God has done for you through Christ.

GRACE IS NOT A LICENSE TO SIN;
IT REMOVES SIN FROM YOUR NATURE.

CHAPTER SIXTEEN

LICENSE TO SIN

LICENSE TO SIN

CHAPTER SIXTEEN

Despite what this section's title might suggest, I promise not to make any James Bond puns, metaphors, or references (again). I chose this title because over the course of my career, I've been told countless times I'm giving people a license to sin. Even now, as I write this book, people argue the ideas presented through teaching complete grace give people a license to sin. They ask, "If God loves us no matter what, then why don't we just sin and have fun?" It's a valid question deserving to be addressed. Did you know in a lot of places you can't even have a yard sale without first getting a license? That seems ridiculous, right? I heard a story once about a little girl who was told she needed to have a temporary restaurant license in order to sell lemonade from a stand in her parents' yard. She literally needed a lemonade license. Did you know you also technically need a license to beg? In most places, you have to become a certified panhandler to legally stand on the street and ask others for money. Thousands of trivial licenses exist. People are supposed to have licenses in order to do the things they already do without a license.

Apparently, we also need a license to sin. You're in luck, though because those who are teaching God's grace are handing these licenses out for free! There's no way people would sin (or continue to sin) without first hearing a message on grace and learning they have a license to do so, right? There's no way someone would have a yard sale without a license! Of course, I'm being sarcastic. The idea God's grace serves as a license to sin is as silly as making a child who's running a lemonade stand apply for a license. Despite arguments to the contrary, we've all done a pretty good job of sinning— with or without the knowledge of God's complete grace.

I get it though. If you've been living under the law and you hear the pure, untainted gospel of grace, then your first reaction might very well be to question the validity of these ideas. On the surface, it seems an understanding that God loves us no matter what we do might lead to even more sin since our sins no longer possess the power to keep God from loving and forgiving us. Now, you might be wondering, "Why live holy if there's nothing that can separate us from God?" Valid question. If God's love is unconditional, then why not just go out and live in sin? God will love us regardless, right? These questions deserve an answer.

The gospel of grace faces the same accusations today it faced when the Apostle Paul was preaching it. Paul preached grace with such passion that people misunderstood his message. Paul taught "where sin abounds, grace abounds much more" (Romans 5:20). People thought his teaching was dangerous in that it could lead others to live however they wanted under the premise that grace was their get-out-of-jail-free card. Now, in all my years as a Christian, I never once thought I could live however I wanted and still receive God's love. Everything I heard in church was pretty much the opposite of the gospel of grace I now know to be true. I didn't have the opportunity to feel free to sin after hearing about God's unconditional love because I left church *feeling* like God's love was conditional. I never once thought I could live in sin and still be accepted by God because I was under so much condemnation. The gospel of grace has to be coupled with a freedom that comes with the knowledge we can still sin without losing God's unconditional love and forgiveness. Otherwise, it's not really Christ's good news. Paul preached grace so strongly people thought he was saying it didn't matter how one lived. They misconstrued his words and took it as a license to sin. People heard Paul's message and thought, "Shall we continue in sin that grace may abound" (Romans 6:1)? Let's look at how

Paul responded to these questions and accusations.

DEAD TO SIN

> *What shall we say then? Shall we continue in sin that grace may abound? Certainly not! How shall we who died to sin live any longer in it? (Romans 6:1-2).*

This is Paul's answer to the license-to-sin argument. When we came to Christ, we died to sin. God gave us a new nature, one that eliminates sin. If you're in Christ, then sin is no longer natural for you. God doesn't just forgive us; He removes sin from our very nature. Romans 6 goes on to declare us free from sin: "Knowing this, that our old man was crucified with Him, that the body of sin might be done away with, that we should no longer be slaves of sin. For he who has died has been freed from sin" (Romans 6:6-7). The "old man" in this passage represents our sinful nature. When Christ died on the cross, He didn't just die *for* you, He died *as* you. He died for what you were. Therefore, your sinful nature has been removed so you might not be a slave to sin but a child of grace.

GRACE IS NOT A LICENSE TO SIN; IT REMOVES SIN FROM YOUR NATURE.

Grace is not a license to sin; it removes sin from your nature. Upon accepting Christ, God's divine nature is within you, and where God reigns, sin cannot survive.

This concept is further explained in 1 John when the word

says, "no one born of God [habitually] practices sin, for God's nature abides in him; and he cannot practice sinning because he is born of God" (1 John 3:9 AMP). It's no longer your nature to sin if you're born of God. When you're "born of God," His nature and spirit dwell within you. Sure, you can still commit the same sins and mistakes you did before coming to Christ, but you'll hate the fact you do those things. You won't receive quite the same satisfaction because it's no longer your disposition to sin.

NEW NATURE

> Grace and peace be multiplied to you in the knowledge of God and of Jesus our Lord, as His divine power has given to us all things that pertain to life and godliness, through the knowledge of Him who called us by glory and virtue, by which have been given to us exceedingly great and precious promises, that through these you may be partakers of the divine nature, having escaped the corruption that is in the world through lust (2 Peter 1:2-4).

People often worry if we remove the threat of the law from people's lives, everyone will run wild. However, God's divine nature lives inside those who come to Christ. The nature of God in you is greater than any outward law placed on you. Upon accepting Christ's gift of grace, your new nature is born of His righteousness and holiness. You no longer need to be governed by an outward set of laws, for you now have the very life of God inside of you, governing from within.

For what the law could not do in that it was weak through the flesh, God did by sending His own Son in the likeness of sinful flesh, on account of sin: He condemned sin in the flesh, that the righteous requirement of the law might be fulfilled in us who do not walk according to the flesh but according to the Spirit (Romans 8:3-4).

The law couldn't produce righteousness. It doesn't nurture obedience. It can't remove your sinful nature. But what the law failed to do, God did by sending His own son. He put your sinful nature to death, nailing it to the cross.

For in Him dwells all the fullness of the Godhead bodily; and you are complete in Him (Colossians 2:9-10).

God isn't trying to get you to conform to a certain set of rules. He simply wants you to live a full life. A life aligning with your new nature. A life is complete in Christ. He just wants you to be yourself. While the law could only attempt to restrain our sinful desires, God's grace gives us the opportunity to abandon our sin altogether. Think about it. How many Christians do you hear scheming on how to get away with more sin? How many people are asking for a message on the best ways to sin and still be good with God? Not many, if any. However, I have met plenty of Christians who want to know how to live free from sin. I've met a lot of people trying to overcome sinful habits. Deep down, we don't want to sin anymore because God gave us a new heart.

> *I will give you a new heart and put a new spirit within you; I will take the heart of stone out and give you a heart of flesh. I will put My Spirit within you and cause you to walk in My statutes, and you will keep My judgments and do them (Ezekiel 36:26-27).*

When you give your life to Christ, He gives you a new heart. He puts a new spirit within you. This new heart wants to live and walk in His holiness. That's its nature. That's your new nature upon accepting Christ. You want to live a life that glorifies God. God gives us His spirit, and with that spirit comes a desire to follow his godly statutes. You don't need a list of rules when you have the Spirit of the living God inside of you as your guide. How helpful is a compass when you have a GPS? The moment you miss a turn, your GPS tells you which way to go and how to correct your mistake. It guides you with step-by-step instructions. God has given us an internal GPS called the Holy Spirit. The Holy Spirit reveals God's will for our lives,

YOU DON'T NEED A LIST OF RULES WHEN YOU HAVE THE SPIRIT OF THE LIVING GOD INSIDE OF YOU AS YOUR GUIDE.

guiding us along. I think often times we place too much trust in the law when we should be letting the Holy Spirit guide our lives.

SIN BRINGS DEATH

I mentioned how much I loved to play Nintendo as a kid, but I also loved to play outside. I didn't have an endless supply of satellite-simulated channels or the World Wide Web to distract me, so I kept busy with basketball, football, and even some street hockey. I remember playing hockey one day right after the movie "The Mighty Ducks" came out. You know a movie was a hit if you have kids in Las Vegas playing street hockey and pretending to be Charlie Conway on the hot asphalt. On this particular day, the sweltering heat and my hockey ambitions were getting the best of me, so I decided to give the "Flying V" formation a break and head inside for something to drink. I went straight to the fridge and swung the door open. I grabbed an ice cold Coca-Cola and rushed back outside. I took a few sips on the sideline, set the can down on the ground, and skated back out on the pavement with my teammates.

After about twenty minutes of knuckle puck action, I returned to my coke for some hydration. I turned the can back, swigging the soda, only this time something was different. The drink wasn't smooth or crisp. It wasn't until my mouth was full of a rather large and chunky sip that I realized an entire colony of ants had marched their way into my can of coke. Hundreds of ants rode projectile waves of coke as I spit out the drink as fast as I could. I thought the coke was going to satisfy my thirst, but instead it left a bad taste in my mouth—literally. This is what sin is like. It's appealing and assures satisfaction. There's a thirst in your soul sin says it can quench, but it doesn't deliver on its promises. It's disappointing, deceiving, and leaves a bad taste in your mouth. And it can sting like ants.

> *What then? Shall we sin because we are not under law but under grace? Certainly not! Do you not know that to whom you present yourselves slaves to obey, you are that one's slaves whom you obey, whether of sin leading to death, or of obedience leading to righteousness? (Romans 6:15-16)*

When you yield to sin, you submit yourself to the author of sin, which brings only death and destruction into your life. Sin **SIN WON'T CHANGE GOD'S HEART TOWARD YOU, BUT IT WILL CHANGE YOUR HEART TOWARD GOD.** affects your conscience. It will rob you of your confidence in God and it will harden your heart toward Him. Sin won't change God's heart toward you, but it will change your heart toward God. Habitual sin can cause the heart to harden and grow cold toward Him. Sin brings death to your mind, body, and soul, therefore, let us not submit ourselves to sin, but to God who sets us free.

The Lord said, "there is no peace for the wicked" (Isaiah 48:22). The word *peace* here is the Hebrew word *shalom*, meaning "peace, prosperity, healing, and wholeness."[16] When you choose to live in sin, you lose your ability to live a whole, peace-filled life. A lot of people inhabit a place where there's enough sin in their lives, to stop them from enjoying the fullness of God, yet there's also enough God in their lives to keep them from enjoying their sin. They're conflicted in their hearts because they're clinging to sin while simultaneously trying to hold on to God. The end result is the absence of peace.

A life without peace isn't easy. "The way of transgressors is hard" (Proverbs 13:15). In this passage the word *hard* refers to a type of difficulty that is "perpetual, constant, and ever flowing."[17] When you choose to cross the boundaries God has set in place, it creates a domino effect. For example, have you ever told a lie that got so big you had to tell another lie just to escape the first one? Before you know it, you find yourself caught up in all kinds of sin. One sin always leads to another. Sin can create large, messy, ongoing problems in our lives.

Even though God forgave us all our past, present and future sins, there are still consequences for sin. This is another reason why grace is far from a license to sin. Choices have consequences. If you choose to live a reckless life, then that life will catch up with you one day. This isn't the result of God punishing you. He's not handing out retribution from on high. Actions hold consequences, good and bad. I've heard people testify that God punished them for drunkenness by causing them to get in a car accident on their way home. This is absurd. They got in an accident because they made a poor choice to drive home drunk. It's the law of sowing and reaping. When you sow to the flesh, you reap the consequences (Galatians 6:7-8). Poor choices produce poor consequences, while good decisions lead to better circumstances.

While sin isn't going to affect God's love and acceptance, God isn't the only person you interact with on a daily basis. Sin is no longer a barrier between you and God, but it can still affect your relationships with others and hurt the people you love the most. You can be forgiven and righteous in God's eyes, yet still be all alone in life due to the choices you have made that hurt those around you. Even under grace, sin still has consequences. It can infect your mind, your emotions, and your relationships with those around you.

It's interesting to note that Paul never tried to motivate people through threats. He didn't try to instill holy living by saying, "God won't bless you anymore…God's won't hear your prayers… or God will punish you if…" Under the New Covenant, the motivation for living holy is different. Paul constantly highlighted our identity in Christ. When you know who you are in Christ, it's easier and more natural to live the abundant life God wants for you. Grace is freedom from sin and a license to live a more whole and peaceful life.

Our belief and trust in God's unconditional
love will cause us to run to Him
even when we fail.

THE SIDE EFFECT OF GRACE

THE SIDE EFFECT OF GRACE

CHAPTER SEVENTEEN

Most things in life come with a set of side effects. The mention of side effects these days always reminds me of prescription drug commercials. One particular commercial I saw listed so many potential adverse effects it was comical. The drug, intended to medicate bipolar disorder, may or may not cause unusual changes in mood or behavior, dizziness upon standing, decreased white blood cells, seizures, trouble swallowing, impaired judgment or motor skills, uncontrollable muscle movements that may become permanent, thoughts of suicide, high fever, stiff muscles, confusion, and last but not least, coma or death. Not to minimize the severity of bipolar disorder, but those side effects sound just as serious, if not worse, than the original problem! So if everything has side effects, what are the side effects of grace? Unlike the side effects of most drugs, the side effects of grace are all good! Thus far, I've tried to define grace, discuss its purpose and design, and highlight its necessity in our lives. Now I'd like to explore what happens in your life when you accept the revelation of God's grace.

LOVE

In 2007, when God began to unfold the gospel of grace to me, I began to experience a newfound love for people. As I continued to unfold and understand grace, I found myself loving people more and more. An effortless and overwhelming love for God and a reenergized compassion for people grew inside of me. It actually took me by surprise because it was such an effortless endeavor. God didn't even speak to me about loving others. Nothing God was showing me about grace specifically mentioned loving others, yet I began to feel this inexplicable love for others. His love and grace for me made me a more loving and graceful person in the most seamless of ways! That's why I believe the most noticeable side effect of grace is a genuine love for people. It's fascinating to me. When I started to focus on God's grace and love, I began to fulfill everything the law set out to do in the first place. God's grace does what the law cannot.

For all the law is fulfilled in one word, even in this: "You shall love your neighbor as yourself" (Galatians 5:14).

Owe no one anything except to love one another, for he who loves another has fulfilled the law. For the commandments, "you shall not commit adultery," "you shall not murder," "you shall not steal," "You shall not bear false witness," "You shall not covet," and if there is any other commandment, are all summed up in this saying, namely, "You shall love your neighbor as yourself." Love does no harm to a neighbor; therefore love is the fulfillment of the law (Romans 13:8-10).

Love is the fulfillment of the law. Loving people starts with a revelation of God's grace. Effortless change is the most permanent change. If you change through your own strength, then it takes constant effort in order to maintain change.

For a long time in my walk with the Lord, it seemed the more I tried to live for Him, the less tolerant I became of others. The more I pursued righteousness, the more judgmental, **EFFORTLESS** critical, and condemning I became. It seemed **CHANGE IS** the holier I felt, the meaner I was. The harder **THE MOST** **PERMANENT** I tried to abide by the rules, the less loving I **CHANGE.** was toward others. If you feel this way, then that's a red flag you're headed in the wrong direction. I think the reason I was judgmental and critical of others was because that's how I thought God was toward me. I was serving a false image of God, and I was becoming just the opposite of who He actually is.

> *Their idols are silver and gold, the work of men's hands. They have mouths, but they do not speak; eyes they have, but they do not see; they have ears, but they do not hear; noses they have, but they do not smell; they have hands, but they do not handle; feet they have, but they do not walk; nor do they mutter through their throat. Those who make them are like them; so is everyone who trusts in them (Psalm 115:4-8).*

Psalm 115 talks about people who worship idols and how those people start to become just like the idols they worship. If your trust is in those idols, then you'll become just like them. We become more like the things we worship. For Christians, we're all being transformed into the image of God we hold in our minds. That's a good thing if you have a clear picture of who God is, but if you have a warped or distorted view of God, then it's extremely dangerous.

If you truly understand and accept God and His grace, then you'll learn to express empathy and compassion toward people when they mess up. If you think God is more condemning than loving, then you'll more readily condemn others. These distorted viewpoints of the nature and character of God cause well-meaning Christians to become more judgmental, critical, and condemning. The characteristics of God you hold in your mind will manifest themselves in your treatment of others. It's

THE CHARACTER-ISTICS OF GOD YOU HOLD IN YOUR MIND WILL MANIFEST THEM-SELVES IN YOUR TREATMENT OF OTHERS.

not because people *want* to be that way. It happens without much planning or effort. The greatest commandment is to love others. If you aren't growing in love for others, then you probably need to reassess your understanding of God.

How can it be that the greatest commandment is to love, yet so many Christians and churches are so lacking in this department? I truly believe this problem is rooted in a misunderstanding of God's character. The majority of people outside of the church think Christians are judgmental and condemning. The reason why they have this perception of Christians is because many Christians view God as being judgmental and condemning. The church has been made into the likeness of a judgmental God that doesn't exist. It's time for us to have a revelation of grace, so we might be made into the likeness of the one, true, loving, and graceful God.

When you begin to understand the grace of God, you start to see who He truly is. And, when we start to see who He truly is, we'll start to look, and live, a lot more like Him (1 John 3:2-3; 2 Corinthians 3:18). When you see "God is love," you become more loving (1 John 4:8). 1 Corinthians 13 describes God's love as patient, kind, long-suffering, and as keeping no record of wrongs. This is the way we need to love people, regardless of their race, religion, sex, creed, or any other circumstance. As we accept God to be truly loving, patient, kind, and not judgmental, we will find these qualities becoming a reality in our hearts.

AS I HAVE LOVED YOU

A new command I give you: love one another. As I have loved you, so you must love one another (John 13:34).

Accept one another, then, just as Christ accepted you, in order to bring praise to God (Romans 15:7).

Be kind and compassionate to one another, forgiving each other, just as in Christ God forgave you (Ephesians 4:32).

We are called to give away the same love, acceptance, and forgiveness we have received from God. Since God's love for us reaches far beyond our actions. Our love for others should extend beyond their shortcomings. Because God forgives every trespass we commit, let us not withhold the gift of forgiveness from those who trespass against us.

The measure of our understanding of God's unmerited love, grace, and acceptance will directly govern the flow of love in our lives. Not only will our love toward God grow, but also our love toward His greatest masterpiece, *people*. When you know God accepts you regardless of what you do, then you begin to extend the same acceptance to others. The more you come to know and experience the depths of God's love for you, the more that same great love will flow through you. From this theology of grace, may we effortlessly come to reflect His image on this earth.

ENDNOTES

FOREWORD

00.   Johnson, edited by Richard L. (2006). Gandhi's experiments with truth : essential writings by and about Mahatma Gandhi. Lanham, MD: Lexington Books.

CHAPTER TWO

1.   http://www.biblestudytools.com/lexicons/greek/kjv/euaggelion.html

2.   https://www.blueletterbible.org/lang/lexicon/lexicon cfm?Strongs=H2483&t=KJV

3.   https://www.blueletterbible.org/lang/lexicon/lexicon.cfm?Strongs=H4341&t=KJV

CHAPTER THREE

4.   http://www.biblestudytools.com/lexicons/greek/kjv/paideia.html

5.   See http://www.merriam-webster.com/dictionary/punishment

6.   See http://www.merriam-webster.com/dictionary/discipline

CHAPTER NINE

7.   http://www.biblestudytools.com/lexicons/greek/kjv/mesites.html

CHAPTER TWELVE

8.   http://www.biblestudytools.com/lexicons/greek/kjv/homologeo.html

CHAPTER THIRTEEN

9.   http://www.biblestudytools.com/lexicons/greek/kjv/makarios.

html

10.   http://www.biblestudytools.com/lexicons/greek/kjv/makarios.
html

11.   http://www.biblestudytools.com/lexicons/greek/kjv/logizomai.
html

12.   http://www.biblestudytools.com/lexicons/greek/kjv/ou-me.html

13.   http://www.biblestudytools.com/lexicons/greek/kjv/teleo.html

CHAPTER FOURTEEN

14.   http://www.biblestudytools.com/lexicons/hebrew/kjv/ed-3.html

CHAPTER FIFTEEN•

15.   https://www.blueletterbible.org/lang/lexicon/lexicon.
cfm?Strongs=G1651&t=KJV

CHAPTER SEVENTEEN

16.   http://www.biblestudytools.com/lexicons/hebrew/kjv/shalowm.
html

17. http://www.biblestudytools.com/lexicons/hebrew/kjv/eythan.html

Made in the USA
Lexington, KY
22 July 2016